SHAH MOHAMMED

Disrupting Perfection

Uncovering the Limitations of Dieter Rams' Design Principles

First edition

This book was professionally typeset on Reedsy.
Find out more at reedsy.com

Contents

Introduction   iv

01 — Good Design is Innovative   1

02 -Good Design Makes a Product Useful   15

03 -Good Design is Aesthetic   28

04 -Good Design Helps a Product Understandable   47

05 -Good Design is Honest   60

06 -Good Design is Long Lasting   76

07 -Good Design is Thorough Down to the Last Detail   85

08 -Good Design is Unobtrusive   95

09 -Good Design is as Little Design as Possible   104

10 -Good Design is Environmentally Friendly   115

Conclusion   121

About the Author   123

Also by Shah Mohammed   125

Introduction

In the field of design, Dieter Rams stands as an iconic figure whose principles have shaped the very essence of modern aesthetics and functionality. His "Ten Principles for Good Design" have been hailed as guiding lights, leading designers through the maze of creativity towards clarity, simplicity, and timeless elegance. Yet, beneath the veneer of perfection lies a paradox — a paradox that begs to be explored, dissected, and understood.

In this book, we embark on a journey that challenges the notion of design perfection embodied by Dieter Rams' principles. We peel back the layers of conventional wisdom, daring to question the very foundations upon which modern design ideology has been built. For within the seemingly flawless framework of Rams' principles, we uncover subtle limitations, overlooked complexities, and uncharted territories that demand our scrutiny.

As we delve deeper into the world of design, we confront the inherent tension between form and function, aesthetics and usability, innovation and tradition. We confront the stark reality that perfection, in its pursuit, may inadvertently breed constraints — constraints that stifle creativity, limit possibilities, and confine the evolution of design.

But this is not a critique born out of disdain or disregard for Rams' legacy. Rather, it is an invitation to engage in a dialogue — a dialogue that celebrates the brilliance of Rams' principles while acknowledging their inherent imperfections. It is a call to embrace the complexities of design, to embrace the messy, the ambiguous, and the uncertain.

In the chapters that follow, we will challenge the status quo, question the assumptions, and redefine the boundaries of design. We will unravel the mysteries of form and function, exploring new frontiers where innovation thrives and creativity flourishes. In doing so, we will discover that true design excellence lies not in perfection but in the willingness to embrace imperfection — to embrace the beauty of the flawed, the unexpected, and the imperfect.

So let us embark on this journey together, with open minds and boundless curiosity. For in the exploration of design's limitations, we may just uncover its greatest strengths — its capacity to inspire, to provoke, and to transform the world around us.

Dieter Rams

Dieter Rams, a luminary in the field of industrial design, stands as a beacon of minimalist elegance and functional beauty. Born in Germany in 1932, Rams rose to prominence during his tenure at Braun, where he served as the company's chief design officer for over three decades. His prolific career not only revolutionized the consumer electronics industry but also left an indelible mark on the broader landscape of design philosophy.

Central to Rams' ethos is the belief that good design should be both aesthetically pleasing and functionally superior. His design principles, often distilled into a concise manifesto of ten precepts, serve as guiding tenets for designers around the world. These principles, born out of Rams' deep reverence for simplicity, clarity, and user-centricity, have become the cornerstone of modern design thinking.

Rams' ten principles for good design are not merely a set of arbitrary rules; they are a distillation of his decades-long exploration into the essence of form and function. From the elegant lines of the Braun SK4 record player to the iconic simplicity of the Braun T3 pocket radio, Rams' designs embody a timeless aesthetic that transcends fleeting trends and fads.

At the heart of Rams' philosophy lies a profound respect for the user — an unwavering commitment to creating products that enhance people's lives in meaningful ways. His insistence on clarity, honesty, and sustainability reflects a deep understanding of the human experience and the role that design plays in shaping it.

Yet, for all their acclaim, the Rams' principles are not without their detractors. Critics argue that his rigid adherence to minimalist ideals may stifle creativity and limit innovation. They question whether his principles are truly applicable in a constantly evolving world. Let's find out.

Dieter Rams' Ten Design Principles

Let us explore each principle:

1. **Good Design is Innovative**: Rams believed that design should push the boundaries of innovation, introducing new ideas, materials, and technologies to enhance the user experience. Innovation, in Rams' view, is the lifeblood of design, driving progress and evolution in both form and function.
2. **Good Design Makes a Product Useful**: Functionality lies at the core of Rams' design philosophy. A product should fulfill its intended purpose effectively and intuitively, enhancing the user's ability to accomplish tasks with ease and efficiency.
3. **Good Design is Aesthetic**: Rams emphasized the importance of aesthetics in design, advocating for simplicity, elegance, and timelessness. Aesthetic appeal, in Rams' view, goes beyond mere decoration; it embodies a sense of harmony and balance that resonates with users on a deeper level.
4. **Good Design Helps a Product Understandable**: Clarity and simplicity are key tenets of Rams' design principles. A product should communicate its function and usage intuitively, without the need for elaborate instructions or explanations.
5. **Good Design is Honest**: Integrity and honesty are essential attributes of good design, according to Rams. A product should be true to its materials, construction, and purpose, free from gimmicks or deceptive features.
6. **Good Design is Long-lasting**: Rams advocated for the creation of products that stand the test of time, both in terms of durability and relevance. Design should eschew fleeting trends and fads, instead

focusing on enduring qualities that withstand the passage of time.

7. **Good Design is Thorough Down to the Last Detail**: Rams believed that every aspect of a product, no matter how small, should be carefully considered and executed with precision. Attention to detail is a hallmark of good design, reflecting a commitment to excellence and craftsmanship.

8. **Good Design is Unobtrusive**: Rams believed that good design should not impose itself upon the user but rather blend seamlessly into the user's environment. Design should be subtle and understated, allowing the user to focus on the task at hand without unnecessary distractions.

9. **Good Design is as Little Design as Possible**: Perhaps the most famous of Rams' principles, this tenet embodies the essence of minimalist design. Design should be stripped down to its essential elements, removing anything that does not contribute to the overall function or aesthetic of the product.

10. **Good Design is Environmentally Friendly**: Sustainability is a core principle of Rams' design philosophy. Designers have a responsibility to minimize environmental impact through thoughtful material selection, manufacturing processes, and product lifecycle management.

These ten principles encapsulate the essence of Dieter Rams' design philosophy, reflecting his unwavering commitment to simplicity, functionality, and user-centricity. In the following chapters, we will delve deeper into each principle, examining its limitations and broader implications for the practice of design in the modern world.

* * *

Who and Why?

This book is intended for designers, creatives, innovators, and anyone interested in understanding the principles of good design and their applications in real-world contexts. Whether you are a seasoned professional seeking to refine your design approach or a newcomer exploring the intricacies of design theory, this book offers valuable insights and perspectives to inspire and inform your creative journey.

Why Should You Read This Book?

1. **Foundational Knowledge**: Understanding the principles of good design is essential for anyone involved in the creation of products, services, or experiences. By delving into the principles articulated by Dieter Rams, one of the most influential designers of the 20th century, readers gain a deeper appreciation for the core tenets that underpin effective design.

2. **Critical Thinking**: Through critiques of each design principle and analysis of examples that challenge conventional wisdom, readers are encouraged to engage in critical thinking and question established norms. This fosters a deeper understanding of the complexities and nuances inherent in the design process, empowering individuals to approach design with greater discernment and creativity.

3. **Inspiration and Innovation**: By exploring the intersections of design theory, practice, and critique, this book serves as a source of inspiration and innovation. Readers are encouraged to draw upon the principles of good design as catalysts for creativity, pushing the boundaries of what is possible and reimagining the future of design in a rapidly changing world.

4. **Holistic Perspective**: Design is inherently interdisciplinary, encompassing aspects of art, engineering, psychology, sociology, and more. This book provides a holistic perspective on design, acknowledging its multifaceted nature and highlighting the interconnectedness of form, function, aesthetics, business objectives, and ethics. By embracing a holistic approach to design, readers gain a deeper appreciation for the impact of design on individuals, communities, and society at large.

In summary, this book is a valuable resource for designers and enthusiasts alike, offering a comprehensive exploration of the principles of good design and their significance in shaping the world around us.

* * *

01 — Good Design is Innovative

Dieter Rams emphasized the principle that "Good Design is Innovative" as a fundamental tenet of his design philosophy. For Rams, innovation was not merely about novelty or trendiness but rather about pushing the boundaries of what was possible to create products that truly enhanced the human experience.

Throughout his illustrious career, particularly during his tenure at Braun, Rams demonstrated a deep commitment to innovation in design. He believed that innovation was essential for staying relevant in a rapidly changing world and for addressing the evolving needs and desires of users.

Rams' approach to innovation was characterized by a blend of visionary thinking and practical application. He sought to introduce fresh perspectives, embrace emerging technologies, and challenge conventional design norms to create products that were both groundbreaking and functional.

The products that emerged from Rams' collaboration with Braun exemplified his dedication to innovative design. From the iconic Braun SK4 record player, with its transparent acrylic casing and sleek lines, to the Braun T3 pocket radio, renowned for its compact form and exceptional sound quality, Rams' designs embodied a harmonious union of form, function, and innovation.

At the heart of Rams' principle of innovation was a belief in the transformative power of design to shape the world for the better. He understood that innovation was not without its challenges and risks, but he remained steadfast in his conviction that it was through innovation that designers could truly make a difference.

Innovation, as Rams envisioned it, was not limited to technological advancements or flashy gimmicks. It was about solving real-world problems, improving quality of life, and creating products that stood the test of time. It required a willingness to question assumptions, challenge the status quo, and embrace experimentation and iteration.

As we explore Rams' principle that "Good Design is Innovative," we delve into the myriad ways in which innovation has the potential to transform the design landscape. From groundbreaking materials and manufacturing techniques to disruptive design thinking methodologies, innovation opens up new possibilities and paves the way for a future where design truly serves humanity in meaningful ways.

Innovation, in the hands of visionary designers like Dieter Rams, becomes not just a means to an end but a guiding principle, a driving force, and a source of inspiration for generations of designers to come. It challenges us to dream big, think boldly, and imagine a world where the possibilities are limited only by our imagination.

The Critique

Critiquing Dieter Rams' principle that "Good Design is Innovative" requires a nuanced examination of both its strengths and limitations. While innovation is undoubtedly a powerful force for driving progress and creativity in design, it also presents several inherent challenges and potential pitfalls:

1. **Overemphasis on Novelty**: The pursuit of innovation may sometimes lead designers to prioritize novelty over practicality and usability. In their quest to create something new and groundbreaking, designers may overlook the fundamental needs and preferences of users, resulting in products that are innovative but ultimately fail to resonate with their intended audience.

2. **Risk of Technological Fetishism**: Innovation often becomes synonymous with the adoption of cutting-edge technologies and materials.

However, a relentless focus on technological innovation can lead to what critic Richard Buchanan refers to as "technological fetishism," where the allure of the latest gadgets and gizmos overshadows considerations of human-centred design and functionality.

3. **The Barrier to Accessibility**: Highly innovative designs may inadvertently create barriers to accessibility for certain user groups. Complex interfaces, obscure features, and unfamiliar design conventions can alienate users who are less technologically savvy or have specific accessibility needs. Highly innovative designs often come with a premium price tag, making them inaccessible to large segments of the population. Designers should consider the affordability and inclusivity of their innovations, ensuring that they are accessible to people from diverse socio-economic backgrounds.

4. **Resistance to Change**: Innovation often disrupts established norms and conventions, challenging users' preconceived notions of how products should look, feel, and function. While disruptive innovation can lead to significant advancements, it can also encounter resistance from users who are resistant to change or unfamiliar with new design paradigms.

5. **Sustainability Concerns**: The relentless pursuit of innovation can have adverse environmental impacts, particularly if it leads to the overconsumption of resources, the production of disposable products, and the generation of electronic waste. Designers must consider the long-term sustainability of their innovations and strive to minimize their ecological footprint.

6. **Innovation for Innovation's Sake**: There is a danger of innovation becoming an end in itself, divorced from its original purpose of addressing real-world problems and improving the human experience. Designers must guard against the temptation to innovate for the sake of innovation, ensuring that their creative endeavours are driven by a genuine desire to create meaningful and impactful solutions.

7. **Lack of emphasis on incremental improvements:** The principle of innovation often places greater emphasis on groundbreaking, disruptive ideas rather than incremental improvements. However, many valuable

design advancements come from small, iterative changes that refine and optimize existing products or processes. Neglecting these incremental improvements may limit the potential for sustained progress.

8. **Disregard for familiarity and user expectations:** Highly innovative designs may challenge users' existing mental models and familiarity with products. While this can lead to breakthroughs, it can also create a steep learning curve and user resistance. Striking a balance between innovation and familiarity is crucial to ensure a positive user experience.

9. **Potential for impracticality or impracticability:** Emphasizing innovation can sometimes lead to designs that are technically impressive but lack practicality or feasibility. Cutting-edge technologies or ideas may not always be viable or economically sustainable. Practical considerations should be carefully balanced with innovative thinking to ensure that designs can be realistically implemented and used.

10. **Neglect of timeless or proven design principles:** Focusing solely on innovation may sideline timeless design principles that have stood the test of time. Tried and tested design principles, aesthetics, and user experience patterns should not be dismissed in favour of pursuing purely innovative ideas. A balance between innovation and adherence to proven design principles is necessary for successful design outcomes.

By critically examining the limitations of this principle, designers can cultivate a more balanced and responsible approach to innovation that prioritizes the needs and well-being of users and society as a whole.

Google Glass

A real-world example that illustrates the critique of "good design is innovative" is the Google Glass project. Google Glass was a highly innovative product that aimed to revolutionize wearable technology by integrating a head-mounted display into a pair of glasses.

The Google Glass concept was lauded for its technological innovation, offering features like hands-free access to informatɪcn, augmented reality capabilities, and a built-in camera. It received significant attention and generated excitement in the tech industry and among early adopters.

However, despite its innovative design, Google Glass faced several challenges that highlighted the limitations of focusing soɭely on innovation:

1. **Privacy Concerns**: One of the primary criticisms lɘveled against Google Glass was its potential to infringe on ɔrivacy rights. The device's built-in camera raised concerns about covert surveillance and unauthorized recording, leading to bans in certain public spaces and establishments.

2. **Social Acceptance**: Google Glass garnered significant attention and curiosity upon its release, but it also faced social stigma and backlash. Users wearing Google Glass were often perceived as "Glassholes," with concerns about the device's intrusion into social interactions and its disconnect from social norms and etiquette.

3. **Design and Aesthetics**: Despite Google's efforts ɪo make Google Glass sleek and fashionable, many users found the devɪce's design clunky and unattractive. Its conspicuous appearance madɘ wearers stand out in public settings, further contributing to social discomfort and reluctance to adopt the technology.

4. **Lack of clear use cases and market fit:** Google Glass was marketed as a versatile device for various applications, ranging from communication to navigation and entertainment. However, it lacɤed clear use cases that resonated with consumers beyond niche industries like healthcare or industrial sectors. The lack of a compelling value proposition limited its market fit and hindered its long-term success.

5. **High Cost and Accessibility**: Google Glass was priɔed at $1,500 upon its initial release, placing it out of reach for the averaɡe consumer. Its high cost combined with limited practical ʋtility made ɪt difficult for users to justify the investment, further impeding widespɽead adoption.

6. **Battery Life and Performance**: Google Glass struggled with limited battery life and performance issues, which hindɘred its usability and practicality in real-world scenarios. Users reported frustration with the

need for frequent recharging and sluggish performance, detracting from the overall user experience.

7. **Lack of Killer Apps**: Despite its innovative technology, Google Glass failed to offer compelling "killer apps" or use cases that would justify its adoption beyond early adopters and tech enthusiasts. The absence of must-have applications limited its appeal and relegated it to a niche product with limited mainstream relevance.

8. **Legal and Regulatory Challenges**: Google Glass encountered legal and regulatory challenges related to its use in various contexts, including concerns about distracted driving and workplace privacy. Governments and regulatory bodies grappled with how to regulate the use of wearable technology like Google Glass, adding another layer of complexity to its adoption.

9. **Cultural and Social Barriers**: Google Glass faced cultural and social barriers in different regions and communities, with some cultures expressing skepticism or hostility towards the intrusive nature of the technology. Cultural norms and attitudes towards privacy and personal space varied widely, influencing the reception of Google Glass in different contexts.

10. **Perception as a Luxury Gadget**: Google Glass was often perceived as a luxury gadget rather than a practical tool for everyday use. Its high price point, limited functionality, and association with tech elitism contributed to its image as a status symbol rather than a transformative innovation accessible to all.

11. **Failure to Address User Feedback**: Despite early enthusiasm and investment in Google Glass, Google faced criticism for its perceived lack of responsiveness to user feedback and concerns. The company's failure to address key issues and iterate on the product in response to user needs contributed to its ultimate demise in the consumer market.

The case of Google Glass serves as a cautionary tale about the limitations of innovation in design. While the device was undeniably innovative in its technology and concept, it failed to address critical concerns such as privacy, social acceptance, design aesthetics, functionality, and accessibility. This underscores the importance of holistic design considerations beyond innovation alone.

Designers must recognize that innovation, while essential, is not sufficient for success. It must be accompanied by careful attention to user needs, societal implications, and ethical considerations to create designs that resonate with users and stand the test of time. By embracing a comprehensive approach to design, designers can navigate the multifaceted challenges and limitations faced by innovative products like Google Glass, ensuring that their creations truly enrich the lives of users and society as a whole.

Volkswagen Beetle

The Volkswagen Beetle, often hailed as one of the most iconic cars in automotive history, presents an intriguing case study that challenges the notion that innovation is the key to success in design.

The Beetle, also known as the "Bug" or the "Type 1," was originally designed by Ferdinand Porsche in the 1930s and later produced by Volkswagen. When the Beetle was launched in the USA in the mid-1950s, the vehicle was not groundbreaking or innovative in terms of its technology or design compared to other cars, yet it achieved remarkable success for several reasons:

1. **Functional and practical design:** Beetle's design prioritized functionality and practicality. It featured a simple, compact body shape that maximized interior space despite its small size. The rear-engine layout and rear-wheel drive allowed for efficient use of space and improved traction, especially in adverse weather conditions. These design choices made the Beetle an economical and versatile vehicle for its time.
2. **Distinctive aesthetics:** The Beetle's design embodied a distinctive aesthetic that has endured for decades. Its round and curvy shape, bulbous fenders, and friendly appearance gave it a unique personality. The Beetle's design was accessible and relatable, resonating with a wide

7

range of consumers and becoming an instantly recognizable symbol.

3. **Durability and reliability:** Beetle's design prioritized durability and reliability. It featured a robust and sturdy construction, capable of withstanding various road conditions. Its air-cooled engine was relatively simple and easy to maintain, contributing to its reputation for longevity and low maintenance costs. The Beetle's design was pragmatic, ensuring that it served its purpose reliably and efficiently.

4. **Affordability and accessibility:** The Beetle was designed to be an affordable and accessible vehicle for the masses. Its simplicity and efficient manufacturing processes allowed for cost-effective production, making it attainable for a large portion of the population. The Beetle's design democratized automobile ownership and provided reliable transportation to many people.

5. **Cultural and historical significance:** The Beetle's design carries significant cultural and historical weight. It represents a symbol of post-war recovery, economic growth, and the "people's car" concept. The Beetle's design reflects an era and a mindset, contributing to its enduring popularity and the affection it holds in the hearts of many enthusiasts.

6. **Emotional Connection**: Beyond its functional attributes, the Beetle fostered a deep emotional connection with drivers and enthusiasts worldwide. Its quirky charm, endearing personality, and memorable advertising campaigns contributed to its status as more than just a mode of transportation but a cherished companion and symbol of individuality.

7. **Heritage and Tradition**: The Beetle benefited from Volkswagen's rich heritage and tradition of automotive craftsmanship and engineering excellence. Its association with the renowned "People's Car" initiative spearheaded by Ferdinand Porsche and Adolf Hitler in the 1930s imbued it with historical significance and cultural resonance that transcended its humble origins.

8. **Versatility and Adaptability**: The Beetle's versatile design allowed it to adapt to various market conditions and consumer preferences over the years. From its origins as a utilitarian "people's car" in post-war Europe to its later iterations as a beloved classic and collector's item, the Beetle

evolved to meet changing tastes and demands.

9. **Global Reach and Enduring Legacy:** The Beetle's global reach and enduring legacy transcend geographic and cultural boundaries. It became synonymous with incremental innovation, reliability, and timeless design, leaving an indelible mark on generations of drivers and car enthusiasts worldwide.

10. **Legacy of Innovation:** While Beetle may not have introduced ground-breaking innovations in its own right, its legacy of innovation lies in its transformative impact on the automotive industry and popular culture. It paved the way for future generations of compact cars and inspired countless designers and engineers to push the boundaries of automotive design and engineering.

The success of the Volkswagen Beetle demonstrates that innovation is not the sole determinant of success in design. While innovation can certainly drive progress and differentiation in the marketplace, other factors play equally crucial roles in shaping the success of a product. The Beetle's enduring popularity serves as a testament to the power of thoughtful design that resonates with users on a deeply emotional and cultural level, transcending mere technological innovation.

Beetle and Incremental Innovations: Dieter Rams' principle that "Good Design is Innovative" often conjures images of groundbreaking, revolutionary innovations that reshape entire industries. However, the success of the Volkswagen Beetle highlights the importance of recognizing the role of incremental innovation in creating differentiation and capturing market share.

Unlike the flashy, disruptive innovations often associated with Rams' principle, the Beetle's success was built on a series of small, incremental improvements that collectively differentiated it from its competitors:

1. **Iterative Design Refinements:** The Beetle underwent numerous iterations and refinements over its production lifespan, each one incorporat-

ing incremental improvements based on user feedback, technological advancements, and market trends. These subtle enhancements, ranging from improved engine performance to enhanced interior comfort, contributed to the Beetle's reputation for reliability and practicality.

2. **Continuous Product Evolution**: Volkswagen continuously evolved the Beetle to keep pace with changing consumer preferences and technological advancements. By introducing new features, trim levels, and design elements over time, the Beetle remained relevant and competitive in a rapidly evolving automotive landscape, ensuring that it retained its appeal to successive generations of drivers.

3. **Customer-Centric Innovation**: The Beetle's incremental innovations were driven by a deep understanding of customer needs and preferences. Volkswagen listened to feedback from drivers, dealers, and automotive experts, identifying pain points and areas for improvement that could be addressed through targeted innovation. By prioritizing customer-centric design principles, Volkswagen ensured that the Beetle remained a compelling choice for consumers seeking affordable, reliable transportation solutions.

4. **Long-Term Sustainability**: The Beetle's emphasis on incremental innovation contributed to its long-term sustainability and endurance in the marketplace. Rather than relying on short-lived fads or technological gimmicks, Volkswagen invested in continuous improvement and refinement, building a loyal customer base and fostering enduring brand loyalty that transcended generations.

In essence, while Dieter Rams' principle emphasizes the importance of bold, visionary innovation in design, the success of the Volkswagen Beetle underscores the equally vital role of incremental innovation in creating differentiation, sustaining competitiveness, and capturing market share. By embracing a balanced approach that incorporates both disruptive breakthroughs and iterative improvements, designers can create products that resonate with users, stand the test of time, and leave a lasting legacy in their respective industries.

Ford Edsel

While the Volkswagen Beetle achieved remarkable success with its simple and functional design, another car launched around the same time took a different approach. Ford introduced the Edsel, accompanied by much anticipation and boasting several technological innovations such as the tele-touch transmission.

The tele-touch transmission, which allowed drivers to shift gears using buttons on the steering wheel, was a notable advancement in automotive technology. It aimed to offer a more convenient and futuristic driving experience. Additionally, the Edsel incorporated other innovative features, including self-adjusting brakes and a rolling dome speedometer.

However, despite its innovative design and promising features, the Edsel faced significant challenges and ultimately failed in the market. Several factors contributed to its lack of success:

1. **High Expectations and Hype**: The Edsel was launched amidst significant anticipation and hype, with Ford investing heavily in marketing and promotion. The lofty expectations surrounding the Edsel created immense pressure for the car to deliver exceptional performance and exceed consumer expectations.
2. **Positioning and Brand Identity Issues**: The Ford Edsel struggled with positioning and brand identity, failing to offer compelling value propositions or differentiate itself effectively from competing products. Its positioning within a non-existent price gap between Ford and Mercury created confusion among consumers and undermined its ability to carve out a distinct identity in the market.
3. **Poor Timing and Economic Climate**: The launch of the Edsel coincided with a period of economic uncertainty and recession in the late 1950s. Consumers were cautious with their spending, and demand for new cars was relatively low. The Edsel's high price point and perceived extravagance made it particularly vulnerable to the economic downturn.
4. **Stiff Competition**: The automotive market in the late 1950s was highly

competitive, with numerous established brands vying for consumer attention. The Edsel faced fierce competition from domestic manufacturers such as General Motors and Chrysler, as well as from imported cars like the Volkswagen Beetle and Toyota Corona.

5. **Design Flaws and Quality Issues**: Despite its innovative features, the Edsel suffered from design flaws and quality control issues that undermined its reliability and durability. Problems with the tele-touch transmission, self-adjusting brakes, and other mechanical components led to frequent breakdowns and costly repairs, tarnishing Edsel's reputation for reliability. Sharing production facilities with the Mercury brand and facing resistance from assembly line workers contributed to inconsistent quality standards, missing parts, and assembly errors that compromised the overall reliability and durability of Edsel vehicles.

6. **Negative Public Perception**: Edsel's unconventional styling and polarizing design elements, such as its distinctive "horse-collar" grille, failed to resonate with consumers. Public perception of the Edsel was mixed, with many viewing it as gaudy, ostentatious, and out of touch with prevailing design trends and consumer tastes.

7. **Misalignment with Consumer Preferences**: The Ford Edsel's development timeline failed to align with shifting consumer preferences and market trends. While initial research indicated a demand for larger cars, evolving economic conditions and rising fuel prices during the development phase shifted consumer preferences towards smaller, more fuel-efficient vehicles. This misalignment between Edsel's design and evolving consumer needs contributed to its failure in the market.

8. **Lack of Dealer Support and Customer Satisfaction**: The rushed rollout of Edsel models to dealerships without adequate quality assurance checks and support systems undermined dealer confidence and customer satisfaction. Dealers faced difficulties addressing customer complaints and warranty issues, leading to negative word-of-mouth and eroding consumer trust in the Edsel brand.

9. **Organizational and Leadership Challenges**: Internal organizational dynamics and leadership decisions also played a role in Edsel's downfall.

The divisional structure and conflicting priorities between Edsel and Mercury management created tension and resistance to collaboration, hindering effective communication, decision-making, and quality control efforts.

10. **Limited Model Variety and Customization**: The Ford Edsel initially launched with a limited range of models and customization options, limiting its appeal to diverse consumer segments with varying preferences and needs. The lack of flexibility in model configurations and trim levels constrained Edsel's ability to attract a wider audience and compete effectively in the marketplace.

11. **Perceived Lack of Innovation**: Despite featuring innovative technological features such as the tele-touch transmission and rolling dome speedometer, the Ford Edsel was perceived by consumers as lacking true innovation and differentiation compared to other contemporary offerings in the automotive market. The perceived lack of innovation diminished Edsel's appeal and undermined its competitive position.

12. **Ineffective Product Differentiation**: Despite efforts to position the Edsel as a premium brand within Ford's lineup, its features and specifications failed to sufficiently differentiate it from other Ford models and competing offerings from rival manufacturers. The lack of compelling differentiation hindered the Edsel's ability to command premium pricing and attract discerning consumers.

In contrast to the success of the Beetle, the Edsel serves as an example of how even innovative features alone cannot guarantee a product's success. Factors such as effective marketing, market conditions, quality control, and price positioning are crucial considerations in achieving commercial viability and meeting consumer expectations. Edsel's story highlights the importance of a holistic approach to design and marketing to create a successful and well-received product.

In conclusion, examining Dieter Rams' principle that "Good Design is Innovative" and its critique reveals a nuanced understanding of the complexities inherent in design theory and practice. While innovation remains a corner-stone of effective design, it is imperative to recognize the inherent challenges and limitations associated with pursuing innovation as the sole driving force behind design endeavours.

The case studies of Google Glass, Ford Edsel and the Volkswagen Beetle offer compelling insights into the diverse manifestations of innovation in design and the multifaceted factors that contribute to the success or failure of innovative products. While Google Glass exemplifies the potential pitfalls of prioritizing innovation without due consideration for user needs, social acceptance, and practicality, the Volkswagen Beetle demonstrates the enduring impact of incremental innovation, customer-centric design, and long-term sustainability.

By embracing a balanced approach that integrates visionary thinking with pragmatic considerations about user needs, desires, and attitudes, designers can navigate the complexities of the design landscape and create products that resonate with users, address real-world problems, and contribute meaningfully to society.

* * *

02 -Good Design Makes a Product Useful

The principle "Good design makes a product useful" encapsulates the fundamental idea that the primary purpose of design is to enhance the functionality and utility of a product for its intended users. This principle, put forward by Dieter Rams, emphasizes the importance of designing products that serve a practical purpose and fulfil user needs effectively and efficiently.

At its core, this principle underscores the notion that design should be driven by functionality rather than mere aesthetics or novelty. It advocates for the creation of products that are intuitive to use, easy to understand, and seamlessly integrate into users' lives.

There are several key aspects to consider when applying this principle to product design:

1. **User-Centred Design:** Good design begins with a deep understanding of user needs, preferences, and behaviours. Designers must empathize with their target audience and strive to create products that address genuine pain points and enhance the user experience.
2. **Functional Simplicity**: Products should be designed with simplicity and clarity in mind, minimizing complexity and unnecessary features that may confuse or overwhelm users. By prioritizing essential functions and streamlining user interfaces, designers can create products that are intuitive and user-friendly.
3. **Efficiency and Effectiveness**: Good design maximizes the efficiency and effectiveness of product usage. This involves optimizing workflows,

minimizing user effort, and eliminating friction points that may impede task completion or detract from the overall user experience.

4. **Accessibility and Inclusivity**: Design should be inclusive and accessible to users of diverse backgrounds, abilities, and levels of expertise. Products should accommodate a range of user preferences and provide accessible features and interfaces that cater to different needs and use cases.

5. **Durability and Reliability**: A useful product is one that is built to last and performs reliably over time. Designers must consider factors such as material quality, durability, and robustness to ensure that products withstand everyday wear and tear and maintain consistent performance throughout their lifecycle.

6. **Seamless Integration into Context**: Products should seamlessly integrate into users' environments and lifestyles, enhancing rather than disrupting their daily routines. Designers should consider the broader context in which products will be used and strive to create cohesive experiences that align with users' expectations and preferences.

7. **Intuitive Navigation and Interaction**: A useful product should have intuitive navigation and interaction mechanisms that allow users to accomplish tasks effortlessly. Clear labeling, logical organization of features, and consistent design patterns help users understand how to interact with the product and access its functionalities efficiently.

8. **Adaptability to User Preferences**: Designing for usefulness involves recognizing and accommodating diverse user preferences and behaviors. Customization options, adjustable settings, and personalized features empower users to tailor the product to their individual needs and preferences, enhancing its utility and relevance in their lives.

9. **Feedback and Error Handling**: Effective design considers the importance of providing meaningful feedback and error handling mechanisms to guide users through the interaction process. Clear feedback signals, informative error messages, and intuitive recovery paths help users understand the outcome of their actions and navigate through potential pitfalls seamlessly.

10. **Sustainability and Environmental Impact**: In today's world, the concept of usefulness extends beyond immediate functionality to encompass broader considerations such as sustainability and environmental impact. Designers should prioritize eco-friendly materials, energy-efficient technologies, and recyclable components to create products that are not only useful but also environmentally responsible and socially conscious.

11. **Scalability and Future-Proofing**: Useful products are designed with scalability and future-proofing in mind, anticipating potential changes in user needs, technological advancements, and market trends. Modularity, upgradability, and interoperability enable products to evolve over time and remain relevant in the face of evolving user expectations and industry developments.

Ultimately, the principle "Good design makes a product useful" emphasizes the importance of designing products that serve a meaningful purpose and add value to users' lives. By focusing on functionality, user-centered design, simplicity, accessibility, durability, and seamless integration, designers can create products that not only meet user needs but also inspire trust, confidence, and satisfaction among users. This principle serves as a guiding framework for designers seeking to create products that are not only aesthetically pleasing but also genuinely useful and impactful in the lives of their users.

The Critique

Critiquing the principle "Good design makes a product useful" involves examining its limitations and potential shortcomings in practical application. While this principle emphasizes the importance of functionality and utility in design, several critiques can be raised:

1. **Subjectivity of "Usefulness"**: The notion of "usefulness" is inherently subjective and context-dependent. What may be considered useful to one user or in one situation may not necessarily apply universally. Designers

may struggle to accurately gauge and prioritize user needs, leading to products that fail to resonate with diverse user groups.

2. **Trade-offs with Aesthetics**: Emphasizing functionality and utility in design may come at the expense of aesthetics and emotional appeal. While a product may excel in terms of usability and practicality, it may lack the visual appeal and emotional resonance that contribute to a positive user experience. Balancing these competing priorities can be challenging for designers.

3. **Limited Scope of Utility**: Focusing solely on utility may result in products that address immediate needs but fail to inspire long-term engagement or loyalty from users. Designers risk overlooking the emotional, aspirational, and experiential aspects of product usage that contribute to a holistic user experience beyond mere functionality.

4. **Assumptions about User Needs**: Designers may make assumptions about user needs and preferences without sufficient empirical evidence or user research. This can lead to design decisions that are based on intuition or personal biases rather than objective data, resulting in products that miss the mark in terms of addressing real user needs.

5. **Inflexibility in Design Solutions**: Prioritizing utility may lead to rigid design solutions that lack flexibility or adaptability to evolving user needs and preferences. Products designed solely for utility may struggle to accommodate changing usage patterns, technological advancements, or shifts in user behavior, limiting their long-term relevance and sustainability.

6. **Overemphasis on Functionality**: Placing too much emphasis on functionality may result in feature bloat or complexity that overwhelms users and detracts from the overall user experience. Designers must strike a balance between providing essential features and minimizing cognitive load to ensure that products remain intuitive and user-friendly.

7. **Neglect of Emotional and Psychological Factors**: The principle of utility overlooks the emotional and psychological dimensions of product design, which play a crucial role in shaping user perceptions and behaviors. Products that evoke positive emotions, foster emotional connections,

and align with users' values and identities are more likely to resonate with users and drive long-term engagement.

8. **Inadequate Consideration of Diversity**: Designing for usefulness may inadvertently overlook the diverse needs, preferences, and abilities of users from different demographic backgrounds, cultures, and contexts. Products that prioritize one-size-fits-all solutions risk excluding marginalized or underrepresented user groups and perpetuating biases and inequities in design.

9. **Potential Trade-off with Creativity and Experimentation**: Prioritizing usefulness may inadvertently stifle creativity and experimentation in design. Designers may feel constrained to adhere to established conventions and practical solutions at the expense of exploring innovative ideas and pushing the boundaries of design. This risk of stagnation may limit the potential for breakthroughs and transformative change in design practice.

10. **Evolution of Utility Over Time**: The notion of usefulness is not static but evolves over time in response to shifting technological advancements, cultural norms, and societal needs. What may have been considered useful in the past may become outdated or irrelevant in the face of changing circumstances. Designers must anticipate and adapt to evolving user expectations and market dynamics to ensure the continued relevance and utility of their products.

11. **User Experience Considerations**: While utility is an important aspect of user experience, it is not the sole determinant of user satisfaction and engagement. A product may be technically useful in terms of fulfilling functional requirements but still fail to deliver a positive user experience due to factors such as poor usability, confusing interfaces, or lack of emotional resonance. Designers must consider the holistic user experience, encompassing not just utility but also usability, aesthetics, and emotional impact, to create truly compelling and meaningful products.

12. **Contextual Nature of Usefulness**: The usefulness of a product is contingent upon the specific context and purpose for which it is intended. A design that is useful in one context may not necessarily be so in

another. Factors such as cultural norms, environmental conditions, user demographics, and situational factors can influence the perceived utility of a product. Designers must consider the context of use and tailor their designs accordingly to ensure optimal usefulness and relevance in diverse settings.

13. **Risk of Over-reliance on Technology**: In the pursuit of utility, designers may prioritize technological features and innovations without considering their true impact on user experience and societal well-being. Over-reliance on technology may lead to dependency, alienation, and unintended consequences such as privacy breaches, data misuse, and algorithmic biases.

14. **Lack of User Empowerment and Agency**: A narrow focus on utility may diminish user empowerment and agency by relegating users to passive consumers rather than active participants in the design process. Products that prioritize utility at the expense of user autonomy may perpetuate paternalistic attitudes and inhibit user creativity, innovation, and self-expression.

15. **Ignorance of Societal and Environmental Contexts**: Designing for utility in isolation may neglect broader societal and environmental contexts in which products are situated. Products that optimize for individual utility may inadvertently contribute to larger systemic issues such as resource depletion, environmental degradation, and social injustice, necessitating a more holistic approach to design that considers the interconnectedness of human, ecological, and technological systems.

While the principle "Good design makes a product useful" underscores the importance of functionality and utility in design, its narrow focus on practical considerations may overlook broader aspects of the user experience and fail to address the complex interplay of user needs, emotions, and societal context. Designers must adopt a more holistic approach that integrates utility with aesthetics, emotion, and user-centred design principles to create truly impactful and meaningful products.

Nokia

One example that exemplifies the critique of the principle "Good design makes a product useful" is that of Nokia, particularly during its dominance in the mobile phone market in the early 2000s.

Nokia's mobile phones were renowned for their practicality, durability, and user-friendly interfaces, embodying the principle of usefulness in design. They prioritized functionality and reliability, offering features that met the basic communication needs of consumers worldwide. Nokia phones were known for their long battery life, sturdy build quality, and intuitive user interfaces, making them popular choices among a wide range of users.

However, as the mobile phone market evolved and consumer preferences shifted towards smartphones with advanced features and touch-screen interfaces, Nokia struggled to keep pace with changing trends. The company's commitment to practicality and utility led to a reluctance to embrace innovative design concepts and user experience enhancements that were gaining traction in the market.

While Nokia's phones remained technically useful in terms of core functionality, they began to lag behind competitors in terms of design aesthetics, user experience, and feature innovation. Consumers increasingly gravitated towards smartphones from brands like Apple and Samsung, which offered sleek designs, intuitive interfaces, and a wide range of apps and multimedia capabilities.

Nokia's failure to adapt to evolving user preferences and market dynamics ultimately led to a decline in its market share and loss of relevance in the mobile phone industry.

This example highlights the limitations of prioritizing usefulness in design without adequately considering factors such as user experience, innovation, and evolving market trends.

Apple AirPods

Apple AirPods serve as a compelling example that challenges the principle that "Good design makes a product useful."

Apple AirPods, despite their commercial success, present a departure from traditional utility-centric design principles. While they seamlessly integrate with Apple's ecosystem and boast innovative features like automatic pairing and touch controls, they also pose usability challenges for certain users. The absence of physical buttons and reliance on touch gestures can lead to accidental triggers and frustration, particularly for individuals with dexterity issues or those accustomed to traditional wired headphones.

Furthermore, AirPods' minimalist design and one-size-fits-all approach compromise functionality in certain scenarios. Users have reported discomfort and difficulty in keeping the AirPods securely in their ears during physical activities or while moving vigorously. This fit-related issue hinders the usefulness of AirPods for individuals seeking a more secure and comfortable fit.

In terms of controls and customization, AirPods offer limited options, primarily relying on touch gestures and voice commands. While contributing to their sleek appearance, this design choice restricts ease of use and customization for some users. Incorporating customizable controls or additional physical buttons could enhance their usefulness and adaptability for individual preferences and scenarios.

Battery life and charging limitations also impact the overall usefulness of AirPods. While sufficient for most users, the need for frequent charging and reliance on a proprietary charging case may inconvenience heavy users, reducing the overall utility of the product.

Additionally, AirPods lack active noise cancellation, limiting their usefulness in noisy environments. Users may struggle to focus on audio content or have clear communication during phone calls in such surroundings. The absence of effective noise isolation features diminishes the overall usefulness of AirPods in certain contexts.

Despite these limitations, AirPods have achieved widespread popularity and success due to Apple's strategic branding efforts and consumer appeal. The complex interplay between design, branding, and user perception underscores the importance of holistic considerations in driving product adoption and market acceptance. While AirPods may not strictly adhere to utility-centric design principles, they exemplify the role of emotional resonance, brand affinity, and lifestyle integration in shaping consumer demand and loyalty. Thus, they serve as a compelling example of how products can achieve commercial success despite deviating from conventional notions of usability and practicality.

Microsoft Zune

One example of a product that was considered useful but failed in the market is the Microsoft Zune media player. Introduced in 2006 as a competitor to Apple's iPod, the Zune offered a range of features and functionality that were aimed at providing a compelling alternative for music enthusiasts. Despite its usefulness, the Zune failed to gain significant traction in the market. Here's a detailed analysis:

1. **Features and functionality:** The Zune offered a range of features that were on par with or even surpassed those of the iPod at the time. It included a large colour screen, wireless syncing, FM radio, and a subscription-based music service. These features made the Zune a useful and feature-rich media player that offered an alternative to the iPod.
2. **User interface and usability:** Zune had a user-friendly interface that allowed users to navigate their music libraries with ease. It introduced the concept of the "Zune Pad," a touch-sensitive pad that provided a unique way to interact with the device. The user interface and usability of the Zune were well-designed, making it an intuitive and useful device for managing and enjoying music.
3. **Integration and ecosystem limitations:** Despite its useful features, Zune faced limitations in terms of its integration and ecosystem. It was

primarily designed to work seamlessly with Microsoft's Zune software and the Zune Marketplace for purchasing and downloading music. This limited compatibility with other platforms and the dominance of Apple's iTunes ecosystem made it less attractive to consumers who were already invested in the Apple ecosystem.

4. **Brand perception and market competition:** Zune faced an uphill battle in terms of brand perception and market competition. Apple's iPod had already established a strong presence and brand loyalty among consumers. The Zune was seen by many as an imitation or copycat of the iPod, which made it challenging to attract users away from the established market leader.

5. **Timing and marketing missteps:** The timing of Zune's launch was also unfavourable. It entered the market several years after the iPod had gained significant market share and popularity. Additionally, the marketing efforts for the Zune were not as effective as those of the iPod, which contributed to lower consumer awareness and interest.

Another key factor that significantly hindered the success of the Microsoft Zune media player was the absence of a comprehensive and user-friendly platform for purchasing songs. In contrast to Apple's iTunes Store, where users could easily and affordably buy songs for just 99 cents each, Microsoft failed to establish a comparable music purchasing ecosystem for the Zune.

The iTunes Store played a crucial role in the explosive success of Apple's iPod. By offering a vast catalogue of songs at an attractive price point, Apple created a seamless and convenient experience for users to discover and purchase music. This integration of hardware and a robust music-purchasing platform propelled the iPod to new heights.

In contrast, Zune lacked a comparable ecosystem that could match the convenience and popularity of the iTunes Store. Microsoft's efforts to establish a competitive music purchasing platform for Zune, known as the Zune Marketplace, fell short in terms of user adoption and the breadth of available content. The limited selection of songs, coupled with a less intuitive user experience, hindered Zune's ability to appeal to music enthusiasts.

The absence of an accessible and well-developed music purchasing platform further exacerbated Zune's challenges. The inability to provide users with an easy and affordable means of acquiring new music restricted the overall usefulness of the device. Consumers were more inclined to choose the iPod, which offered seamless integration of hardware, software, and an extensive music catalogue.

Google+

Another example of a product that faced challenges in the market despite its usefulness is Google+. Launched in 2011, Google+ aimed to compete with social media giants like Facebook and Twitter by offering users a new platform for social networking and content sharing.

Google+ introduced several innovative features and functionalities that differentiated it from existing social media platforms. These included Circles, which allowed users to organize their connections into different groups and control the sharing of content with specific audiences. Hangouts offered users the ability to participate in group video calls and chat sessions, fostering real-time communication and collaboration. Additionally, Google+ is integrated seamlessly with other Google services such as Gmail, YouTube, and Google Photos, providing users with a unified and interconnected online experience.

From a utility standpoint, Google+ offered valuable features and capabilities that addressed user needs for social networking, communication, and content sharing. Circles provided users with greater control over their online interactions, while Hangouts facilitated meaningful connections and collaboration among users. The integration with other Google services enhanced the platform's functionality and convenience, making it an appealing option for users seeking an alternative to existing social media platforms.

However, despite its usefulness, Google+ struggled to gain widespread adoption and failed to compete effectively with Facebook and Twitter. Several factors contributed to its limited success in the market:

1. **Network Effects:** Facebook and Twitter had already established large and active user bases by the time Google+ was launched. The network effects inherent in social media platforms made it difficult for Google+ to attract users away from established networks where their friends, family, and contacts were already active.

2. **Brand Perception:** Google+ faced challenges in establishing a distinct identity and brand image separate from other Google products and services. The platform's association with Google may have led some users to perceive it as a secondary or supplementary offering rather than a primary social networking destination.

3. **User Experience and Interface Design:** While Google+ introduced innovative features, some users found the platform's interface and user experience to be complex and confusing compared to other social media platforms. The learning curve of navigating Circles and understanding privacy settings has deterred some users from fully embracing the platform.

4. **Privacy Concerns:** Google's data collection practices and privacy policies came under scrutiny, raising concerns among users about the security and privacy of their personal information on Google+. The perception of inadequate privacy protections may have discouraged some users from engaging with the platform and sharing content openly.

5. **Lack of Content and Engagement:** Despite its initial momentum and user sign-ups, Google+ struggled to sustain user engagement and activity over time. The platform faced challenges in generating compelling content and fostering meaningful interactions among users, leading to stagnation and eventual decline in user interest.

In summary, while Google+ offered useful features and capabilities that addressed user needs for social networking and communication, it failed to overcome significant challenges in the market. The platform's inability to attract and retain users, establish a distinct brand identity, and differentiate itself from competitors ultimately contributed to its demise. The case of Google+ serves as a cautionary tale about the complexities of competing in the social media landscape and the importance of addressing broader considerations beyond utility in driving product adoption and success.

In conclusion, the principle "Good design makes a product useful" emphasizes functionality and utility but may overlook broader aspects of user experience, innovation, and market dynamics. Examples like Nokia's decline, Apple AirPods' usability challenges, Microsoft Zune's ecosystem limitations, and Google+'s struggle for adoption illustrate the complexities of balancing utility with user needs, brand perception, and competitive landscapes. Designers must adopt a holistic approach, integrating utility with aesthetics, user experience, and societal context to create impactful and successful products.

* * *

03 -Good Design is Aesthetic

Dieter Rams emphasized the importance of aesthetics in design as a means of enhancing user experience and enriching everyday life. According to Rams, aesthetics encompass more than just visual appeal; they also include aspects such as form, proportion, harmony, and simplicity.

Simplicity and Minimalism: Central to Rams' philosophy is the idea of simplicity and minimalism. He advocated for designs characterized by clean lines, uncluttered forms, and timeless elegance. Well-designed products, according to Rams, should exhibit balance and harmony, engaging users on both visual and tactile levels.

Honesty and Integrity: Rams stressed the importance of honesty and integrity in aesthetic design. He rejected superficial ornamentation and unnecessary embellishments in favour of authenticity and clarity of expression. By prioritizing essential elements and eliminating excess, designers could create products that resonate with users and stand the test of time.

Timelessness in Design: Rams advocated for designs with a timeless quality, enduring beyond passing trends and fads. He believed that well-designed products should remain relevant and appealing regardless of changing tastes or technological advancements, emphasizing enduring qualities such as elegance, balance, and harmony.

Quality Craftsmanship: Rams emphasized the importance of quality craftsmanship in aesthetic design. He highlighted the use of high-quality materials, precision manufacturing techniques, and attention to detail to create products that exude excellence and durability. Quality craftsmanship enhances a product's aesthetic appeal and instills confidence in its reliability and longevity.

Functionality Above All: Aesthetic considerations should never compromise functionality, according to Rams. He argued that truly aesthetic design seamlessly integrates form and function, enhancing the usability and effectiveness of a product. Aesthetic elements should serve a purpose beyond mere decoration, contributing to the overall user experience and satisfaction.

In summary, Dieter Rams' principle of "Good Design is Aesthetic" underscores the intrinsic connection between aesthetics, functionality, and user experience in design. Aesthetic considerations play a crucial role in shaping perceptions, fostering emotional engagement, and enhancing usability, ultimately contributing to the overall success and longevity of a product.

Now, let's explore criticisms of this principle and its limitations in contemporary design practices.

The Critique

While aesthetics undoubtedly play a significant role in the design, a critical analysis reveals certain complexities and considerations. Here's a detailed critique of this principle:

1. **Subjectivity in Aesthetics**: Aesthetic preferences vary greatly among individuals and cultures. What one person finds aesthetically pleasing, another may not. Rams' emphasis on simplicity and minimalism may not resonate with everyone, leading to a narrow interpretation of aesthetic value.

2. **Exclusion of Emotional and Experiential Design**: Aesthetic design, as defined by Rams, often overlooks the emotional and experiential aspects of design. Designers should consider how products make users feel and the overall experience they provide, beyond just their visual appearance.

3. **Lack of Consideration for Diversity and Inclusion**: Rams' aesthetic principles may inadvertently perpetuate exclusionary design practices by

favouring a particular aesthetic ideal that may not be inclusive of diverse perspectives, cultures, and identities. Design should embrace diversity and prioritize inclusivity to create products that resonate with a broader range of users.

4. **Risk of Stagnation and Lack of Innovation**: Strict adherence to Rams' aesthetic principles of minimalism may stifle creativity and innovation in design. Designers may feel constrained by the need to adhere to predefined aesthetic norms, limiting experimentation and exploration of new ideas and approaches.

5. **Limited Relevance in Rapidly Changing Contexts**: In today's fast-paced world characterized by rapid technological advancements and changing cultural trends, Rams' timeless aesthetic principles may become outdated or less relevant. Designers must adapt to evolving contexts and embrace new aesthetic paradigms to remain responsive to changing user needs and preferences.

6. **Cultural and Contextual Relevance**: Aesthetic preferences are deeply influenced by cultural and contextual factors. Rams' aesthetic principles, rooted in Western design traditions, may not resonate with cultures and contexts outside of Western societies. Designers must consider the cultural and contextual relevance of aesthetic choices to create designs that are inclusive and respectful of diverse perspectives.

7. **Perpetuation of Design Hierarchies**: Rams' aesthetic principles have been criticized for perpetuating hierarchies within the design industry, privileging certain design approaches and aesthetics over others. This can limit opportunities for underrepresented designers and perpetuate exclusionary practices within the design community.

8. **Ethical Implications of Aesthetic Choices**: Aesthetic decisions in design can have ethical implications, particularly concerning issues such as cultural appropriation, representation, and social justice. Designers must critically evaluate the ethical implications of aesthetic choices and strive to create designs that are ethically responsible and socially conscious.

While Dieter Rams' principle of "Good Design is Aesthetic" offers valuable insights into the importance of aesthetics in design, it also has notable limitations and may not fully encompass the complexities and nuances of contemporary design practice. Designers must critically evaluate aesthetic principles in the context of broader considerations of usability, functionality, inclusivity, sustainability, and innovation to create truly impactful and meaningful designs.

Superficial Ornamentation and Embellishments: Dieter Rams' rejection of superficial ornamentation and unnecessary embellishments in favour of authenticity and clarity of expression reflects a commitment to simplicity, functionality, and honesty in design. While this principle resonates strongly in certain contexts, there are scenarios where it may not universally apply or appeal to all consumers.

One key consideration is the diverse range of consumer preferences and cultural contexts. While some individuals may appreciate minimalist designs that prioritize clean lines and understated elegance, others may gravitate towards designs that feature embellishments, intricate details, and ornamental elements. These embellishments can evoke feelings of luxury, craftsmanship, and exclusivity, catering to the tastes and sensibilities of certain consumer segments.

Furthermore, specific product categories and industries may inherently lend themselves to ornamental design elements. For example, luxury goods such as watches, jewellery, and fashion accessories often incorporate ornate detailing and embellishments as a symbol of prestige and craftsmanship. In these contexts, superficial ornamentation may be integral to the brand identity and perceived value of the product, resonating strongly with consumers who seek aspirational and indulgent experiences.

Moreover, cultural and historical factors play a significant role in shaping aesthetic preferences and design sensibilities. In some cultures, ornate and decorative designs hold deep symbolic meanings and cultural significance, reflecting traditions, rituals, and societal norms. In such contexts, minimalist design principles may be perceived as sterile or lacking in character, failing to resonate with consumers who value richness, symbolism, and tradition in design.

Timeless Design Limitations: While Dieter Rams advocates for timeless design principles, the reality of consumer behaviour often diverges from this notion. In many cases, designs that create trends and capture attention through novelty and innovation can experience significant commercial success, even if they deviate from timeless aesthetics.

Consider a scenario where several companies adhere to minimalist, timeless design principles for a particular product category. Their products may indeed exude elegance and timelessness, but they risk blending into the market without making a distinct impression on consumers. However, if a competitor introduces a product with a bold, curvy design featuring multiple curves, it has the potential to stand out prominently amidst the sea of minimalist offerings.

This contrast in design approach can spark intrigue among consumers, who may perceive the company behind the curvy design as innovative and daring. The product's unique aesthetic can capture attention and differentiate the brand, leading to a surge in sales and market recognition.

Designs that defy convention and provoke curiosity have the potential to reshape perceptions, elevate brand recognition, and drive significant commercial success, even if they deviate from traditional notions of timeless aesthetics.

iMac G3: The iMac G3, introduced by Apple in 1998, is a prime example of a product that deviated from traditional notions of timeless aesthetics but still made a significant impact in the market. Unlike minimalist designs favoured by Dieter Rams, the iMac G3 embraced bold colours, playful curves, and translucent plastics, setting it apart from the conventional computer designs of the time.

The iMac G3's unconventional design, spearheaded by Jony Ive, challenged industry norms and captured the imagination of consumers with its innovative and approachable aesthetics. Its vibrant colour options, including Bondi Blue, Tangerine, and Strawberry, appealed to a broader audience beyond traditional tech enthusiasts, making computing more accessible and appealing to everyday users.

Despite its departure from timeless design principles, the iMac G3's distinctive appearance served as a visual statement of Apple's commitment to creativity, innovation, and user-friendly technology. The all-in-one design, with its integrated monitor and compact form factor, also contributed to its popularity among consumers seeking streamlined computing solutions for home and office use.

Moreover, the iMac G3's design reflected Apple's broader branding strategy, positioning the company as a pioneer in the digital age and a champion of forward-thinking design. Its iconic silhouette and bold color palette became synonymous with the Apple brand, reinforcing its reputation for innovation and pushing the boundaries of conventional design aesthetics.

Ultimately, while the iMac G3 may not adhere to timeless design principles in the traditional sense, its bold and memorable aesthetics played a pivotal role in revitalizing Apple's image, redefining the consumer computing experience, and laying the foundation for future design innovations across the tech industry.

Here are a few more examples that illustrate the limitations of timeless aesthetics:

1. **Fashion Industry**: In the fashion industry, trends change rapidly, and what is considered fashionable and desirable today may become outdated tomorrow. Designers often experiment with bold colors, patterns, and styles to capture consumer attention and remain relevant in a competitive market. While timeless pieces such as little black dresses or tailored suits endure, the industry thrives on innovation and novelty, challenging the notion of timeless aesthetics.

2. **Technology Products**: In the field of technology products, such as smartphones and laptops, consumer preferences evolve quickly, driven by advancements in technology and changing lifestyle trends. Design elements that were once considered timeless may appear outdated as new features and design trends emerge. Companies like Apple continuously iterate their product designs to stay ahead of the curve and appeal to

modern consumers, challenging the notion of timeless aesthetics in technology.

3. **Automotive Design**: Automobiles offer another example of the limitations of timeless aesthetics. While classic car designs may evoke nostalgia and admiration for their timeless beauty, contemporary automotive design often emphasizes innovation, aerodynamics, and cutting-edge technology. Car manufacturers regularly introduce new models with sleek, futuristic designs to appeal to consumers' desire for innovation and performance, shifting away from traditional notions of timeless aesthetics.

4. **Home Decor and Interior Design**: Home decor and interior design trends evolve with changing tastes, lifestyles, and cultural influences. While timeless design principles such as clean lines and neutral colours endure, consumers often seek out new and innovative design concepts to personalize their living spaces and reflect their individual styles. Interior designers experiment with eclectic combinations, bold accents, and unique furnishings to create spaces that feel contemporary and inviting, challenging the idea of timeless aesthetics in home decor.

5. **Consumer Electronics**: The consumer electronics industry is characterized by rapid innovation and technological advancements. Products such as televisions, audio systems, and home appliances undergo frequent design updates to incorporate the latest features and functionalities. While minimalist designs may appeal to some consumers, others may prefer products with expressive, avant-garde aesthetics that reflect their personality and lifestyle choices.

In summary, while timeless aesthetics hold value in design for their enduring appeal and universal appeal, they are not without limitations. Design trends evolve, consumer preferences shift, and industries innovate to stay competitive in dynamic markets. As such, designers must strike a balance between timeless principles and contemporary trends to create products that resonate with modern consumers and stand the test of time in an ever-changing world.

Dyson Airblade V Hand Dryer

The Dyson Airblade V hand dryer, known for its inncvative technology and efficient hand-drying capabilities, has been praised for its functionality and performance. However, its aesthetic design has received mixed reviews and serves as an example of how aesthetics alone do not guarantee the success or perception of good design. Here's a detailed analysis:

1. **Functional design:** The Dyson Airblade hand dryer is designed with a focus on functionality and efficiency. It utilizes a high-speed, powerful air stream to quickly dry hands, reducing the need for paper towels and contributing to sustainability. The design prioritizes the primary function of the product, which is to dry hands effectively and efficiently.

2. **Utilitarian aesthetics:** The aesthetic design of the Dyson Airblade hand dryer is often described as utilitarian. It features a slim, sleek profile with a stainless steel finish, reflecting a contemporary industrial design. While this aesthetic may be appealing to some users who appreciate simplicity and functionality, it may not evoke the same level of visual allure or emotional connection as more ornate or visually striking designs.

3. **Lack of visual warmth:** One critique of the Airblade's aesthetic design is the perceived lack of visual warmth or personality. Its clean lines and industrial appearance can come across as cold or sterile to some users. Utilitarian aesthetics, while suitable for commercial environments, may not resonate as strongly with users seeking a warmer or more visually engaging design.

4. **Contextual considerations:** The Airblade's aesthetic design must also be considered within its intended context. As a commercial hand dryer primarily found in public restrooms and high-traffic areas, the design focuses more on durability, ease of maintenance and cleanliness rather than solely on visual aesthetics. In this context, the emphasis on functionality and hygiene may outweigh the need for intricate or visually striking design elements.

5. **Perception of premium quality:** Despite mixed reviews of its aesthetic

design, the Dyson brand's reputation for innovative and high-quality products has influenced the perception of the Airblade hand dryer. The brand's association with cutting-edge technology and performance may compensate for any perceived shortcomings in the purely aesthetic aspects of the design.

The Dyson Airblade hand dryer exemplifies a product that is highly functional and successful in its intended purpose, despite mixed reviews regarding its aesthetic design. While the utilitarian aesthetics and lack of visual warmth may be seen as drawbacks, the product's focus on functionality, efficiency, and brand reputation has contributed to its market success.

Dyson Airblade V Hand Dryer

Toyota Prius

Another example of a product that challenges the principle of "Good Design is Aesthetic" is the Toyota Prius, particularly its earlier generations. The Prius, introduced in the late 1990s, revolutionized the automotive industry by popularizing hybrid technology and fuel efficiency. However, its design has often been criticized for its unconventional appearance and lack of aesthetic appeal.

1. **Innovative technology:** The Toyota Prius introduced groundbreaking hybrid technology to the automotive industry, offering significant improvements in fuel efficiency and reduced emissions. Its design is primarily focused on accommodating the advanced hybrid drivetrain, battery, and aerodynamic enhancements. The emphasis on technological innovation takes precedence over purely aesthetic considerations.

2. **Polarizing exterior design:** The exterior design of the Prius has been a subject of controversy and mixed opinions. Its unique shape, characterized by a sloping roofline, wedge-shaped profile, high rear deck, elongated cabin, angular lines, and distinctive rear end, is intended to optimize aerodynamics and improve fuel efficiency. However, this design choice has been polarizing, with some praising its futuristic and distinct appearance, while most find it unconventional or even unattractive.

3. **Interior functionality:** The interior of the Prius is designed with functionality and efficiency in mind. It offers practical features and controls that prioritize usability and accessibility. However, the aesthetic design of the interior has been criticized for its use of plastic materials and a lack of premium finishes or luxurious touches commonly found in other vehicles in its price range.

4. **Balancing form and function:** The Prius design showcases the challenge of balancing form and function. While its design choices prioritize aerodynamics and fuel efficiency, critics argue that more attention could have been given to creating a visually appealing exterior and interior that align with contemporary automotive design trends and consumer

expectations.

5. **Perception and brand identity:** Despite criticisms of its design, the Toyota Prius has achieved significant success and has become a recognizable icon in the hybrid vehicle market. Its unique design has contributed to its distinct brand identity and differentiation from traditional gasoline-powered cars. The perceived environmental benefits and fuel efficiency of the Prius have influenced consumer perception and acceptance, overshadowing some of the aesthetic critiques.

The Prius demonstrates that aesthetics alone do not determine the perception of good design, as other factors such as technological innovation, environmental impact, and brand identity can significantly influence consumer acceptance and market success.

Amazon Kindle E-reader

Another example of a product that achieved massive success despite not being aesthetically pleasing is the original Amazon Kindle e-reader. When it was first introduced in 2007, the Kindle's design was functional but not particularly stylish or visually appealing. Its appearance was characterized by a utilitarian aesthetic, featuring a plastic body with physical buttons and a grayscale e-ink display.

While the original Kindle lacked the sleekness and elegance typically associated with premium electronic devices, it revolutionized the way people read and consumed digital content. The Kindle offered users access to a vast library of e-books in a portable, lightweight device, enabling them to carry thousands of titles with them wherever they went.

The success of the Kindle can be attributed to several key factors beyond its aesthetics:

1. **Functionality**: Despite its simple design, the Kindle excelled in functionality, providing users with a seamless reading experience optimized

for long-form content. Its e-ink display replicated the look of printed text, reducing eye strain and enhancing readability, particularly in bright sunlight.

2. **Convenience**: The Kindle's wireless connectivity allowed users to purchase and download e-books directly from the Amazon Kindle Store, eliminating the need for physical bookstores or computer connections. This convenience factor appealed to avid readers and contributed to the device's widespread adoption.

3. **Affordability**: The Kindle was competitively priced compared to traditional printed books and other e-readers on the market at the time. Its affordability made it accessible to a broad range of consumers, democratizing access to digital literature and expanding the e-book market.

4. **Content Ecosystem**: Amazon's robust ecosystem of digital content, including e-books, newspapers, and magazines, complemented the Kindle's hardware, offering users a vast selection of reading materials to choose from. The seamless integration between the Kindle device and Amazon's content platform enhanced the overall user experience and incentivized continued usage.

Despite its utilitarian design, the original Amazon Kindle resonated with consumers seeking a convenient, portable, and affordable way to enjoy digital reading. Its success paved the way for subsequent iterations of the Kindle and contributed to the widespread adoption of e-books and digital reading devices worldwide. The case of the Kindle demonstrates that while aesthetics are important, they are not always the sole determinant of a product's success, particularly when functionality, convenience, and affordability are prioritized.

Segway Personal Transporter

The Segway, a self-balancing electric scooter, garnered significant attention and admiration for its innovative design, pleasing aesthetic appeal and potential to revolutionize personal transportation. However, despite its aesthetic appeal and practicality, it did not achieve widespread adoption. Here's a detailed analysis:

1. **Unique design:** The Segway featured a sleek and futuristic design with a self-balancing mechanism that allowed users to effortlessly navigate through urban environments. Its compact size, minimalistic frame, and intuitive controls contributed to its aesthetic appeal, making it an eye-catching and visually appealing mode of transportation.
2. **Practicality and functionality:** The Segway offered benefits such as ease of use, manoeuvrability, and eco-friendly electric operation. It provided an efficient and convenient alternative to walking or using traditional modes of transportation, particularly in urban areas with short commutes. Its functionality and potential for reducing traffic congestion and carbon emissions made it an attractive option for personal mobility.
3. **High price point:** The Segway's high price was a significant factor in its market failure. The initial cost of the device was relatively steep, limiting its accessibility to a niche market of early adopters and businesses. The price point created a barrier to mass-market adoption, as potential customers were hesitant to invest in a relatively expensive personal transportation device.
4. **Safety concerns and regulatory challenges:** The Segway faced safety concerns and regulatory challenges in various jurisdictions. Some cities and countries restricted its use on sidewalks or public spaces due to potential accidents or conflicts with pedestrians. These limitations hindered the Segway's usability and market expansion, reducing its appeal to potential consumers.
5. **Market positioning and target audience:** The Segway struggled to define its target audience and market positioning effectively. While it had

potential applications for urban commuting, tourism, and industrial use, it did not align clearly with specific user needs or preferences. This lack of focus made it challenging to generate widespread demand or establish a distinct market segment for the product.

6. **Perception and social acceptance:** Despite its innovative design and functionality, the Segway faced challenges related to social acceptance and perception. It was often associated with a perception of laziness or impracticality, as its adoption was primarily limited to leisurely tours or niche business applications. Overcoming these negative perceptions proved to be a significant hurdle in achieving broader market acceptance.

The Segway Personal Transporter is an example of a product with great aesthetic appeal and practicality but failed to achieve mass-market success. Factors such as its high price point, safety concerns, regulatory challenges, undefined target audience, and negative social perceptions contributed to its market failure. While the Segway showcased innovation in personal transportation, these challenges demonstrate that aesthetics and functionality alone are not sufficient for a product's success, and market positioning, pricing, and social acceptance are equally critical factors to consider.

Juicero Juicer

One example of a product that aligned with Dieter Rams' aesthetic principles yet faced significant challenges in the market is the Juicero Juicer. Juicero was introduced in 2016 with much fanfare, promising to revolutionize the way people consume cold-pressed fresh juice at home. The juicer boasted a sleek, minimalist design characterized by clean lines, high-quality materials, and an intuitive user interface, aligning closely with Rams' emphasis on minimalistic aesthetics, simplicity, and functional design.

Juicero aimed to simplify the juicing process by offering pre-packaged, organic produce in convenient, single-serving packs. Users could insert these packs into the juicer, which would then extract fresh juice at the press of a button. The product's streamlined design and emphasis on ease of use appealed to health-conscious consumers seeking convenient solutions for incorporating fresh fruits and vegetables into their diets.

Despite its aesthetically appealing design and innovative approach to juicing, Juicero encountered several challenges that ultimately led to its downfall. One of the primary issues was its exorbitant price tag, with the initial cost of the juicer exceeding $400 and individual juice packs priced at a premium. The high cost of entry limited the product's accessibility and appeal to a niche market segment, hindering its mass-market adoption.

Additionally, Juicero faced criticism and controversy surrounding the perceived value of its product. Investigations revealed that the juicer's proprietary technology, which purportedly ensured optimal juice extraction, could be bypassed by manually squeezing the juice packs with bare hands, rendering the expensive hardware redundant. This revelation undermined consumer confidence in the product and raised questions about its efficacy and utility.

Furthermore, Juicero's business model relied heavily on subscription-based revenue streams tied to the sale of proprietary juice packs, which further limited its appeal and sustainability. The company struggled to justify the ongoing costs associated with its product ecosystem, especially in the face of cheaper alternatives available in the market.

Ultimately, despite its adherence to Dieter Rams' aesthetic guidelines and principles of functional design, Juicero failed to gain traction and ultimately ceased operations in 2017. The case of Juicero serves as a cautionary tale about the importance of balancing aesthetics with practicality, affordability, and market viability in product development. While aesthetics play a crucial role in shaping consumer perceptions and desirability, they must be complemented by robust business strategies and value propositions to ensure long-term success in the competitive marketplace.

Casper Mattress

We have seen that 'Aesthetic' design, as defined by Rams, often overlooks the emotional and experiential aspects of design. A relevant example is the Casper mattress.

Casper disrupted the traditional mattress industry by focusing not only on the aesthetic appeal of its products but also on the overall experience and emotional connection with customers. Here's how Casper exemplifies this approach:

1. **Comfort and Functionality**: Casper mattresses are designed with a primary focus on comfort and functionality. The brand uses innovative materials and technology to create mattresses that offer optimal support, pressure relief, and temperature regulation, ensuring a restful and rejuvenating sleep experience. While aesthetics are important, Casper prioritizes the physical comfort and performance of its mattresses to enhance the user experience.

2. **Customer-Centric Design**: Casper places a strong emphasis on understanding the needs and preferences of its customers. The brand conducts extensive research and gathers feedback to inform its product design and development process. By prioritizing customer insights and listening to user feedback, Casper ensures that its mattresses are tailored to address specific pain points and deliver a superior sleeping experience tailored to individual preferences.

3. **Brand Identity and Storytelling**: Casper has cultivated a distinct brand identity centred around the concept of better sleep and wellness. Through engaging storytelling and branding initiatives, Casper communicates its commitment to improving the quality of sleep and promoting overall well-being. The brand's messaging emphasizes the emotional benefits of a good night's sleep, such as improved mood, productivity, and overall health, resonating with consumers on a deeper level beyond aesthetics alone.

4. **Unboxing Experience and Trial Period**: Casper enhances the customer

experience by offering a unique unboxing experience and a generous trial period. Upon delivery, customers are greeted with elegantly packaged mattresses that are easy to unpack and set up. This unboxing ritual adds an element of excitement and anticipation, turning the mattress delivery into a memorable and enjoyable experience. Additionally, Casper offers a risk-free trial period that allows customers to test the mattress in the comfort of their own home, providing peace of mind and confidence in their purchase decision.

5. **Community Engagement and Customer Support**: Casper fosters a sense of community and connection with its customers through various engagement initiatives and exceptional customer support. The brand leverages social media, content marketing, and community events to interact with customers, share sleep-related tips and insights, and create a sense of belonging among its audience. Casper's responsive customer support team ensures that customers feel valued and supported throughout their entire journey, further strengthening the emotional bond with the brand.

Casper challenges the notion that good design is solely aesthetic by prioritizing the emotional and experiential aspects of design in its mattress products and brand experience. By focusing on comfort, functionality, customer-centricity, storytelling, and community engagement, Casper creates meaningful connections with customers and delivers a sleep experience that goes beyond just visual appeal.

In conclusion, while Dieter Rams' principle of "Good Design is Aesthetic" emphasizes the importance of aesthetics in design, it also faces criticisms and limitations in contemporary design practices. While aesthetics are crucial, they must be balanced with considerations of functionality, inclusivity, user-centricity, business factors, innovation, and cultural relevance to create truly impactful and meaningful designs that resonate with diverse audiences and stand the test of time.

DISRUPTING PERFECTION

* * *

04 -Good Design Helps a Product Understandable

D ieter Rams' principle "Good Design Helps a Product Under-standable" underscores the importance of clarity, simplicity, and intuitiveness in design to facilitate user understanding and interaction with a product. This principle emphasizes the role of design in communicating functionality, purpose, and usage instructions effectively, thereby enhancing the overall user experience.

At its core, this principle advocates for designs that prioritize user compre-hension and ease of use, minimizing confusion, ambiguity, and the need for complex instructions or manuals. A well-designed product should convey its intended purpose and functionality intuitively, allowing users to interact with it confidently and without friction.

Rams believed that good design should eliminate barriers to understanding and empower users to navigate and engage with a product effortlessly. This involves considerations such as clear labeling, logical organization of features and controls, intuitive feedback mechanisms, and ergonomic considerations to accommodate users of varying abilities and preferences.

Moreover, Rams emphasized the importance of consistency and coherence in design language and visual cues to reinforce user understanding and familiarity across different contexts and interactions. Consistent use of symbols, icons, colors, and typography can help users interpret and navigate interfaces, controls, and informational displays more effectively.

In essence, "Good Design Helps a Product Understandable" advocates for designs that prioritize user needs, cognitive ergonomics, and intuitive inter-action paradigms. By fostering clarity, coherence, and ease of comprehension, well-designed products can empower users to derive maximum utility and satisfaction from their interactions, ultimately enhancing the overall user experience and fostering long-term engagement and loyalty.

The Critique

Critically analyzing Dieter Rams' principle "Good Design Helps a Product Understandable" reveals its limitations in contemporary design practice.

1. **Assumes Homogeneous Users**: The principle may overlook the diversity of users and their varying levels of familiarity with technology. What is understandable to one user may not be to another, especially across different demographic groups, cultural backgrounds, or levels of digital literacy.
2. **User Familiarity Challenges:** The principle of making a product under-standable assumes a certain level of user familiarity and context, which may not always be the case. Understandable is a subjective experience influenced by various factors such as cultural background, knowledge, and familiarity with similar products. What may be considered under-standable for experienced users or professionals in a particular field may not be the same for novice users or those with limited technical knowledge. Designers cannot guarantee universal understanding due to the diverse user base they cater to.
3. **Contextual Challenges**: The complexity of certain products and tech-nologies makes it challenging to achieve complete understandability. In an effort to incorporate advanced features and functionalities, products can become increasingly intricate and difficult to comprehend. Those products and technologies cannot be simplified without sacrificing their core features. Striving for simplicity may result in oversimplification, limiting the capabilities and effectiveness of the product.

4. **Overemphasis on Simplicity**: While simplicity is often desirable, it should not come at the expense of functionality or innovation. In some cases, overly simplistic designs may limit creativity, flexibility, or the ability to accommodate diverse user needs and preferences.

5. **Limited Consideration of Cognitive Load**: While the principle advocates for understandable design, it may not sufficiently address the cognitive load placed on users, especially in systems with extensive information or complex interactions. Designers must consider not only clarity but also the cognitive demands imposed on users.

6. **Dynamic User Expectations**: User expectations and design trends evolve over time, challenging the notion of what constitutes "understandable" design. What may be considered intuitive today may become outdated or insufficient tomorrow, necessitating ongoing adaptation and iteration in design practice.

7. **Information hierarchy and organization:** While organizing information is crucial for understandability, it can be challenging to determine the most effective hierarchy and organization for diverse user needs. Different users may have different information preferences and priorities, making it difficult to create a one-size-fits-all approach to information organization. Additionally, overly rigid information structures may limit user exploration and hinder intuitive understanding.

8. **Diverse user backgrounds:** Users come from various educational back-grounds, and their knowledge and skill levels differ significantly. Some users may be experts in the field, while others may be novices or have limited familiarity with similar products. Designing for such a diverse user base requires careful consideration of varying levels of technical understanding and ensuring that the design accommodates different levels of expertise.

9. **Cognitive abilities and age-related considerations:** Users' cognitive abilities can vary, including factors such as memory, attention span, and problem-solving skills. Additionally, the age of users can impact their interaction with the product. Designers must account for cognitive limitations and design interfaces and interactions that are clear and easily

comprehensible for users across different age groups, including older adults who may have specific usability challenges.

10. **Accessibility considerations:** Inclusive design is essential to address the needs of users with disabilities. Visual impairments, hearing impairments, mobility limitations, and other accessibility requirements introduce additional complexity to the design process. Providing alternative modalities, support for assistive technologies, and adhering to accessibility guidelines are crucial for ensuring that the product is understandable and usable by individuals with diverse abilities.

11. **Learning Curve vs. Intuitiveness**: Striving for immediate understandability may overlook the potential benefits of a learning curve. While intuitive design is valuable, some products or systems may offer advanced functionality that requires users to invest time in learning. Balancing intuitive interaction with opportunities for exploration and mastery is essential for creating engaging and rewarding user experiences.

Considering the above factors increases the inherent complexity of the design. Designers must strike a delicate balance between providing a comprehensive experience for users with diverse backgrounds while keeping the design simple and intuitive.

In addition to the aforementioned factors, it is important to consider that some individuals actually appreciate cognitive load and enjoy some challenges when using a product. This is because putting effort into understanding and figuring out a product can create a sense of ownership and value, known as the endowment effect. In certain cases, complexity can be necessary and even desirable.

1. **Cognitive engagement and sense of achievement:** Some users derive satisfaction and a sense of accomplishment from overcoming challenges and investing cognitive effort in understanding/using a product. When a design presents them with complex tasks or features that require problem-solving, exploration, and learning, they may find the expe-

rience more rewarding. The act of unravelling the intricacies of a product can enhance their engagement and overall perception of its value.

2. **Personal investment and endowment effect:** The endowment effect refers to the psychological bias where individuals place a higher value on items they perceive as their own. When users invest time, effort, and mental energy into understanding a complex product, they tend to develop a sense of ownership and attachment to it. This feeling of ownership can lead to a higher perceived value and satisfaction with the product, even if it initially presented challenges.

3. **Targeting specific user segments:** Complexity can be intentional in products designed for specific user segments, such as hobbyists, professionals, or enthusiasts who seek a deeper level of engagement and complexity. In these cases, the product is tailored to meet the needs and preferences of a niche audience that appreciates and values the cognitive load associated with understanding and utilizing the product's advanced features.

Tesla Model S Touchscreen

One example that challenges the principle that "Good Design Helps a Product to be Understandable" is the Tesla Model S touchscreen interface.

While Tesla's touchscreen interface offers a wealth of features and functionalities, its design has been criticized for its complexity and lack of intuitive usability. The large touchscreen serves as the primary interface for controlling various aspects of the vehicle, including navigation, media playback, climate control, and vehicle settings.

1. **Electric vehicle technology:** The Tesla Model S was one of the first electric cars to achieve significant range capabilities and performance, challenging the limitations of traditional internal combustion engines. The complex technology underlying the electric drivetrain, battery

management, and regenerative braking required users to understand and adapt to a new way of driving and charging their vehicles.

2. **Complexity**: The Tesla Model S touchscreen interface presents users with a multitude of options and settings, which can be overwhelming and difficult to navigate, especially for new users. The sheer number of features and menus can lead to confusion and frustration, detracting from the overall user experience.

3. **Learning Curve**: The touchscreen interface requires users to invest time in learning its intricacies and navigating through its menus and submenus. While some users may appreciate the depth of features and customization options, others may find the learning curve steep and discouraging, particularly those accustomed to more traditional physical controls in vehicles.

4. **Autopilot and driver-assistance features:** Tesla's Autopilot system, which offers advanced driver-assistance features, presented another layer of complexity for users. Understanding how to engage and disengage Autopilot, interpreting its capabilities and limitations, and adapting to the dynamic interaction between the driver and the autonomous features required a learning process.

5. **Driver Distraction**: Interacting with a touchscreen while driving can pose safety risks by diverting the driver's attention away from the road. Unlike physical knobs and buttons that offer tactile feedback and can be operated without looking, touchscreen controls often require visual attention and precise finger gestures, increasing the potential for driver distraction and accidents.

6. **Inconsistent User Experience**: Tesla's touchscreen interface has undergone multiple software updates and revisions over time, resulting in changes to the layout, functionality, and user interface elements. These frequent updates can lead to inconsistencies in the user experience, as users may encounter new features or changes in functionality without adequate guidance or explanation.

7. **Accessibility Concerns**: The touchscreen interface may present accessibility challenges for users with disabilities or impairments, such as

visual or motor limitations. Without alternative input methods or robust accessibility features, some users may struggle to effectively interact with the interface, limiting their ability to control essential vehicle functions.

Despite the complexity, the Tesla Model S garnered a devoted following of early adopters and tech enthusiasts who valued its environmental benefits, cutting-edge technology, and sleek design. The appeal of owning a vehicle that pushed the boundaries of automotive innovation outweighed the initial learning curve associated with its operation.

The success of the Tesla Model S demonstrates that consumers are willing to embrace complex usability if it comes with significant technological advancements and benefits that outweigh the initial challenges. Tesla's commitment to continuous software updates, improved user experience, and ongoing customer education also played a role in helping users adapt to the complex functionalities of their electric vehicles. As a result, the Model S became a popular choice among electric car enthusiasts and played a crucial role in driving the wider adoption of electric vehicles in the automotive industry.

Raspberry Pi

Raspberry Pi is a credit-card-sized single-board computer developed for educational purposes and hobbyist projects. The Raspberry Pi offers a wide range of capabilities, allowing users to build and experiment with various electronic projects and programming.

1. **Complexity and Learning Curve**: Raspberry Pi is not your typical plug-and-play device. It requires users to have some level of understanding of electronics, programming, and computer architecture. For newcomers, the Raspberry Pi can be daunting due to its complexity and steep learning curve. However, this complexity is precisely what appeals to its target audience of enthusiasts, hobbyists, educators, and tinkerers who relish

the challenge of exploring new technologies and learning new skills.

2. **Devoted Following**: Despite its initial learning curve, the Raspberry Pi has cultivated a devoted following of users who appreciate its versatility and potential. The Raspberry Pi Foundation's commitment to education and community engagement has fostered a vibrant ecosystem of enthusiasts who share knowledge, collaborate on projects, and push the boundaries of what is possible with the device. This sense of community and camaraderie encourages users to embrace the challenges posed by Raspberry Pi and embark on creative and innovative endeavours.

3. **Endowment Effect**: As users invest time and effort in understanding the Raspberry Pi and creating projects with it, they develop a sense of ownership and attachment to the device. The endowment effect amplifies their appreciation for its capabilities and potential, leading to a deeper sense of satisfaction and pride in their creations. This emotional connection further reinforces the Raspberry Pi's appeal and contributes to its enduring popularity among its user base.

4. **Empowerment Through Learning**: Raspberry Pi empowers users to explore and experiment with technology in ways that were previously inaccessible to them. By providing an affordable and accessible platform for learning and experimentation, the Raspberry Pi democratizes access to computing and fosters digital literacy among users of all ages and backgrounds. The journey of understanding and mastering the Raspberry Pi becomes a transformative experience for many, igniting a passion for technology and innovation that extends far beyond the device itself.

The Raspberry Pi challenges traditional notions of simplicity and easy understanding by embracing complexity and fostering a culture of learning and exploration. Its success lies not in its simplicity, but in its ability to inspire curiosity, creativity, and collaboration among its users, ultimately empowering them to unlock their full potential in the world of technology and computing.

Dark Souls

Dark Souls is known for its challenging gameplay, intricate level design, and punishing difficulty. While many modern video games focus on accessibility and ease of play, Dark Souls deliberately embraces complexity and high difficulty levels as part of its core design philosophy. Here's how it illustrates the concept:

1. **Challenging gameplay:** Dark Souls is designed to provide a demanding and immersive gaming experience. It features intricate combat mechanics, strategic decision-making, and intense boss battles that require precise timing, skilful execution, and perseverance. The game intentionally presents players with difficult challenges and forces them to learn from their mistakes and adapt their strategies, fostering a sense of accomplishment and satisfaction upon overcoming obstacles.

2. **Depth and exploration:** Dark Souls offers a rich and intricate world to explore, filled with hidden paths, secrets, and lore. The game encourages players to engage in thorough exploration, discovery, and experimentation to uncover its intricate lore and interconnected world. The complexity of the game world and its mechanics deepens the sense of immersion and reward for players who invest time and effort into understanding its intricacies.

3. **Dedicated player community:** Dark Souls has garnered a dedicated and passionate fan base who appreciate the game's complexity and demanding nature. These players seek out challenging experiences and value the sense of achievement and personal growth that comes from overcoming difficult obstacles. They actively engage with online forums, share strategies, and exchange tips, forming a community that celebrates the complexity and depth of the game.

While Dark Souls may not appeal to all players due to its high difficulty and complex gameplay, it has garnered critical acclaim and a devoted following precisely because of its challenging nature. The game's intentional embrace

of complexity and the satisfaction derived from mastering its mechanics contribute to its appeal for a specific segment of gamers who value a demanding
and rewarding experience.

It is important to note that while complexity and cognitive load can be
valuable in certain cases, it is essential to strike a balance. Designers must
consider the target audience, their motivations, and the context in which
the product will be used. Providing appropriate levels of complexity, clear
guidance, and support for users who may not appreciate or benefit from
excessive cognitive load remains crucial in creating a successful and usable
product.

Manual Espresso Machines

Manual espresso machines require users to have a deeper understanding of
the coffee brewing process, and they offer more control and customization
options compared to automated or capsule-based machines.

1. **Coffee enthusiasts and connoisseurs:** Manual espresso machines appeal
   to coffee enthusiasts who value the process and artistry of brewing
   espresso. These individuals appreciate the complexity and control that
   manual machines offer, allowing them to experiment with different
   variables such as grind size, water temperature, and extraction time
   to achieve their desired flavour profiles. The involvement and engagement required to master the manual brewing process are often seen as
   rewarding and enjoyable by coffee aficionados.
2. **Customization and personalization:** Manual espresso machines provide
   users with a high level of customization and personalization. Users can
   adjust various parameters to tailor the taste, strength, and texture of their
   espresso shots. This level of control allows individuals to create their
   own unique coffee experiences and experiment with different brewing
   techniques to achieve their preferred results. The complexity of the
   manual process can be seen as an opportunity for customization and

personal expression.

3. **Ritual and experience:** For some users, the process of using a manual espresso machine becomes a ritual and an experience in itself. From grinding the coffee beans to tamping the grounds and manually control-ling the extraction, every step requires attention and skill. This hands-on approach can create a sense of satisfaction and engagement, elevating the coffee brewing process to a more meaningful and enjoyable activity.

While manual espresso machines require more time, effort, and skill compared to their automated counterparts, they cater to a specific segment of coffee lovers who value the complexity, control, and artistry of espresso preparation. These individuals find joy in the learning process, the hands-on experience, and the ability to create customized and high-quality espresso shots.

It's important to note that not all coffee drinkers may appreciate the complexity of manual espresso machines. Many individuals prefer the convenience and simplicity of automated machines or capsule systems. The key is to provide options that cater to different preferences and skill levels, allowing users to choose a coffee brewing method that aligns with their desired level of complexity and involvement.

Herman Miller's Aeron Chair

The Aeron chair is an excellent example of a consumer product that achieved tremendous success despite its complexity of usability. Designed by Bill Stumpf and Don Chadwick, the Aeron chair revolutionized office seating with its innovative features and ergonomic design. Here's how it exemplifies the concept:

1. **Ergonomic complexity:** The Aeron chair introduced a level of ergonomic sophistication that was unprecedented in office seating. It incorporated features such as adjustable armrests, lumbar support, tilt and recline mechanisms, and a mesh seat and backrest that provided optimal comfort

and support for long hours of sitting. While these features offered enhanced ergonomics, they also required users to familiarize themselves with the various adjustments and settings to optimize their seating experience.

2. **Customization options:** The Aeron chair offered users a range of customization options to suit their individual preferences and body types. The chair came in different sizes to accommodate various heights and weights, and users could select from a variety of materials and finishes. While the ability to customize the chair allowed for a tailored experience, it also added complexity in terms of selecting the right configuration for individual users.

3. **Learning curve and adjustment period:** Due to its unique design and ergonomic complexity, users often required some time to adapt and find their optimal seating position in the Aeron chair. The various adjustments and settings provided versatility but also demanded users invest time and effort in understanding and fine-tuning their seating experience.

Despite the complexity of usability, the Aeron chair became a remarkable success and an iconic symbol of office furniture design.

The Aeron chair's success can be attributed to its ability to address the growing demand for ergonomic solutions in the office environment. While the complexity of its usability may have initially posed a challenge, users recognized the long-term benefits and value it provided in terms of comfort, productivity, and well-being. The Aeron chair's impact on the office furniture industry and its continued popularity even after several decades speak to its design excellence and the enduring appeal of its ergonomic complexities.

In conclusion, the exploration of various examples, including the Tesla Model S touchscreen interface, Raspberry Pi, Dark Souls, manual espresso machines, and Herman Miller's Aeron Chair, underscores the nuanced relationship between complexity and usability in design. While simplicity and ease of understanding are often prioritized in design principles, these examples demonstrate that complexity can also hold value, especially when it aligns with user preferences, fosters engagement, or enables advanced functionality. Designers must carefully balance the level of complexity to meet the needs and expectations of diverse user segments while ensuring usability, accessibility, and satisfaction. Ultimately, the success of a product lies in its ability to provide meaningful experiences that resonate with users, whether through simplicity, customization, or the embrace of complexity.

* * *

05 -Good Design is Honest

Dieter Rams advocated for honesty in design, emphasizing transparency, integrity, and sincerity in the creation of products. Here's a detailed explanation of this principle:

1. **Transparency**: Honest design involves clear and transparent communication of a product's purpose, functionality, and characteristics. Design elements should convey accurate information to users, enabling them to make informed decisions and understand what to expect from the product. A product should be true to its materials, construction, and purpose, free from gimmicks or deceptive features.

2. **Integrity**: Design integrity entails a commitment to truthfulness and authenticity throughout the product's lifecycle. This includes using high-quality materials, adhering to ethical manufacturing practices, and ensuring that the product performs as advertised without misleading or deceptive claims.

3. **Sincerity**: Honest design reflects genuine consideration for the needs, values, and experiences of users. It involves empathizing with users' perspectives and designing products that genuinely address their concerns, desires, and aspirations. Sincere design fosters trust and credibility between the user and the product, leading to positive user experiences and long-term satisfaction.

4. **Clarity and Simplicity**: Honest design is characterized by clarity and simplicity, with design elements that are straightforward, understandable, and devoid of unnecessary complexity or obfuscation. By prioritizing

simplicity and clarity, designers can facilitate intuitive interactions and foster meaningful engagement with the product

5. **Ethical Considerations**: Honest design also encompasses ethical considerations, such as respecting user privacy, promoting sustainability, and minimizing environmental impact. Designers have a responsibility to consider the broader societal implications of their products and ensure that they align with ethical principles and values.

In summary, Dieter Rams' principle of "Good Design is Honest" underscores the importance of transparency, integrity, sincerity, and ethical considerations in design. Honest design builds trust, fosters positive user experiences, and contributes to the overall integrity and credibility of the product and its brand.

Now, let's delve into the critique of this principle.

The Critique

Let's delve into the critique of the principle of "Good Design is Honest":

1. **Subjectivity in Truthfulness**: One limitation of the principle is that truthfulness can be subjective and influenced by individual perspectives and biases. What one designer or company considers honest and transparent may not align with the expectations or interpretations of users. This subjectivity can lead to discrepancies in how honesty is perceived and evaluated in design.

2. **Marketing and Branding Tactics**: In practice, the pursuit of honesty in design may be compromised by marketing and branding strategies aimed at creating aspirational or emotional connections with consumers. Companies often employ persuasive techniques, storytelling, and brand narratives that may embellish or exaggerate the qualities of a product, deviating from strict honesty in favor of engaging and captivating consumers.

3. **Complexity and Hidden Features**: Some products, particularly in technology and electronics, may contain complex features or functionalities that are not immediately apparent to users. While designers may argue that these features enhance the product's utility or performance, their presence may challenge the principle of honesty if users are unaware of or misled about their existence.

4. **Omissions and Concealment**: Designers may intentionally omit or conceal certain information about a product to prioritize simplicity or aesthetic appeal. While this approach may enhance the user experience in some cases, it can also be perceived as a lack of transparency or honesty, especially if crucial details about the product's functionality or limitations are withheld from users.

5. **Perception vs. Reality**: Honesty in design can be challenged by discrepancies between users' perceptions and the actual capabilities or qualities of a product. Even if designers aim to communicate honestly, users may interpret design elements or product claims differently, leading to misunderstandings or misconceptions about the product.

6. **Ethical Dilemmas and Trade-offs**: Balancing honesty in design with ethical considerations and business objectives can pose challenges for designers and companies. Ethical dilemmas may arise when designers must weigh the potential benefits and risks of disclosing certain information about a product, especially if transparency could negatively impact sales or competitive advantage.

7. **Cultural and Societal Context**: The definition of honesty in design can vary across different cultural and societal contexts. What may be considered acceptable or expected in one culture may be perceived differently in another. Designers must navigate these cultural nuances and sensitivities to ensure that their products resonate with diverse audiences while maintaining integrity and transparency.

8. **Evolving Standards**: Standards of honesty and transparency in design evolve over time in response to changing consumer expectations, regulatory requirements, and industry practices. Designers must remain vigilant and adaptable to emerging trends and developments in ethical

design standards to ensure that their products meet evolving societal expectations.

9. **Competitive Pressures**: In highly competitive markets, there may be pressure to highlight the positive aspects of a product while downplaying its limitations or shortcomings. This competitive environment can incentivize designers and marketers to engage in tactics that prioritize sales and market share over complete transparency and honesty.

10. **Confidentiality and Proprietary Information**: In certain industries, particularly technology and innovation-driven sectors, companies may need to protect confidential or proprietary information about their products. While transparency is valued, disclosing sensitive information about proprietary technologies or trade secrets could undermine a company's competitive advantage or intellectual property rights.

11. **Regulatory Constraints**: Regulatory requirements and industry standards may impose limitations on the extent to which product information can be disclosed or communicated to users. Compliance with legal and regulatory frameworks often involves striking a balance between transparency, consumer protection, and commercial interests, which may necessitate trade-offs in terms of the level of disclosure.

12. **User Understanding and Comprehension**: Users may have varying levels of understanding, comprehension, and literacy when it comes to technical or specialized information about products. Designers must consider the cognitive capabilities and information processing abilities of their target audience when communicating product details, ensuring that information is accessible, digestible, and meaningful to users.

While the principle of "Good Design is Honest" emphasizes the importance of transparency, integrity, and sincerity in design, its practical application can be complex and multifaceted, requiring careful consideration of ethical, cultural, and business factors. Designers must strive to strike a balance between honesty and other design objectives while prioritizing the interests and experiences of users.

Peak-end Rule

Imagine three bottles — Bottle A, which has a cylindrical shape; Bottle B, with a wider base and a converging shape towards the neck; and Bottle C, with a smaller base and a diverging shape towards the neck. Bottle A represents an honest representation of the time it takes to fill the bottle. However, Bottle B and Bottle C utilize design elements that create different perceptions.

When filling Bottle B, the narrower top gives users the impression of a faster filling process as the water level in the top half rises quickly due to the narrower shoulders. This design choice manipulates the user's perception, making them believe that the water is filling up more rapidly. On the other hand, Bottle C, with its wider top, creates the illusion of a slower filling process. Users may feel that the container is filling up slowly, causing potential dissatisfaction.

A similar scenario can be observed with shampoo bottles. It is crucial that users do not feel that the shampoo is being emptied faster than expected, as this may lead to negative experiences and potentially prompt them to switch to another brand. Bottle C, with its diverging shape from the base, may create the perception of fast consumption. After a few days of usage, the visible drop in the shampoo level can mislead users into thinking that the product is being used up quickly. In contrast, Bottle B, with its wider base and narrower shoulder, gives the illusion of slower consumption. The gradual decrease in the level with each use is not as noticeable, fostering a sense of satisfaction and trust in the brand.

These examples highlight how design choices can intentionally manipulate users' perceptions to enhance their overall experience. While Bottle A represents honesty, the needs and preferences of users often align with designs like Bottle B or other variations.

In these cases, designers employ subtle manipulations in the design to influence user perceptions and create a more positive experience. While this may deviate from complete transparency, it serves the purpose of enhancing user satisfaction and engagement.

Treadmills: Another real-world example where the Peak-End Rule is employed to prioritize user welfare despite deviating from the principle of "Good Design is honest" is in the design of exercise equipment, particularly treadmills.

Many treadmills come equipped with features such as virtual running courses, scenic routes, or entertainment screens to make the exercise experience more engaging and enjoyable for users. However, the design of these features often involves subtle manipulations to influence users' perceptions and overall satisfaction.

For instance, during a workout session on a treadmill with a virtual running course feature, the treadmill may simulate running through picturesque landscapes or famous landmarks. The scenery may change dynamically based on the user's pace or incline settings, providing a visually stimulating and immersive experience.

The Peak-End Rule comes into play at the conclusion of the workout session. Instead of abruptly ending the virtual course experience, the treadmill may gradually transition to a calming and relaxing scene, such as a serene beach or tranquil forest, during the cooldown period.

This deliberate design choice aims to create a positive and memorable end to the exercise session, leaving users feeling satisfied and fulfilled. By ending on a high note, the treadmill enhances the overall exercise experience and encourages users to return for future workouts.

While this design approach may involve some degree of manipulation by creating an artificially pleasant end to the workout, it ultimately serves the welfare of users by promoting regular exercise and healthy habits. The use of the Peak-End Rule in this context demonstrates how design decisions can be tailored to optimize user well-being and satisfaction, even if they deviate from complete transparency.

Notifications: Platforms like Facebook, Instagram, and Twitter utilize various psychological techniques to encourage users to spend more time on their platforms and engage with content. While these techniques may not always align with complete transparency, they are implemented with the intention of enhancing user experience and fostering social connections.

One prominent example is the use of intermittent reinforcement through notifications. Social media platforms strategically send notifications to users based on algorithms that predict when they are most likely to engage with the app. These notifications are often designed to be unpredictable and intermittent, similar to the principles behind slot machines in casinos.

By delivering notifications inconsistently and at unexpected times, social media platforms capitalize on the psychological principle of variable reward schedules. Users become conditioned to anticipate notifications and experience a rush of excitement or pleasure when they receive them, prompting them to check their phones and engage with the platform more frequently.

While this approach may not be completely transparent about the platform's intentions to increase user engagement, it aims to enhance user welfare by fostering social connections, facilitating communication, and providing entertainment. Social media platforms argue that these features enable users to stay connected with friends and family, discover relevant content, and participate in online communities.

However, critics argue that the use of such psychological tricks can contribute to addictive behaviours, distract users from real-world interactions, and even negatively impact mental health. Despite these concerns, social media platforms continue to balance the implementation of engagement-boosting features with efforts to promote responsible usage and user well-being.

It's important to note that these examples highlight the complexity of design decisions and the need to consider various factors, such as user psychology, perception, and overall experience. While honesty remains a fundamental principle in design, there are instances where a certain level of manipulation or shaping of user perceptions can be employed to create better user experiences.

Designers must carefully consider the implications of these choices and balance transparency with the desired user experience. By managing user expectations, providing a positive experience, and ensuring ethical practices, designers can build trust and loyalty among users.

Gamification

Another example where the principle of "Good Design is Honest" may not be applicable is in the field of gamification and behavioural design. Gamification involves incorporating game-like elements into non-game contexts to motivate and engage users. Behavioural design focuses on influencing user behaviour through strategic design choices. In these cases, designers may employ techniques that nudge users towards desired actions, even if it involves a degree of manipulation.

For instance, many fitness apps and wearable devices use gamification elements to encourage users to engage in physical activity. They may include features like progress tracking, badges, challenges, and social competition to motivate users to exercise more. While these elements can be effective in promoting healthy behaviours, they may not always provide a completely honest representation of the user's progress or the effort required to achieve certain milestones.

In some instances, the gamification elements may exaggerate achievements or use notifications to create a sense of urgency or social pressure. This can lead users to perceive their progress or activity levels in a more positive light or feel compelled to engage in certain behaviours. While these techniques can be motivating, they may not align with strict notions of honesty.

This manipulation is needed to encourage users to lead an active, healthy life by maintaining their interest and motivation in engaging with exercise and fitness activities. Many individuals struggle to maintain consistent exercise routines due to various factors such as lack of motivation, time constraints, or competing priorities. By incorporating gamification elements into fitness apps and wearable devices, developers aim to address these barriers and provide users with incentives to stay committed to their fitness goals.

Gamification elements such as progress tracking, badges, challenges, and social competition tap into intrinsic human motivations such as achievement, competition, and social connection. These elements create a sense of accomplishment and satisfaction as users track their progress, earn rewards, and compete with friends or other users. Additionally, they provide immediate feedback and reinforcement, which can reinforce positive behaviours and encourage users to continue exercising regularly.

Moreover, gamification helps to make the fitness experience more enjoyable and engaging, transforming exercise from a mundane task into a fun and interactive activity. By introducing elements of play and competition, users are more likely to feel motivated and invested in their fitness journey, leading to increased adherence and long-term behaviour change.

While gamification may not always provide a completely honest representation of a user's progress or the effort required to achieve certain milestones, it serves as a powerful tool for promoting positive health behaviours and improving overall well-being. The psychological manipulation inherent in gamification is necessary to overcome barriers to exercise adherence and empower individuals to take control of their health and fitness.

Nest

Another example of a product that employs psychological manipulation while deviating from the principle of honesty in design is the Nest Learning Thermostat. The Nest Thermostat uses a combination of sensors, algorithms, and user interactions to create a personalized heating and cooling schedule for the home.

One of its key features is the ability to adjust the temperature automatically based on user behaviour and preferences. The thermostat tracks user patterns, such as when they are home or away, and adjusts the temperature accordingly to conserve energy and optimize comfort.

While this functionality can contribute to energy savings and convenience, it also involves subtle manipulation of user behaviour. The thermostat learns from user adjustments and patterns over time, creating the impression that it is adapting to the user's preferences. However, the extent to which the thermostat truly learns and adapts may be overstated, as it relies on predetermined algorithms and user input to make adjustments.

Additionally, the Nest Thermostat utilizes a sleek and intuitive interface that encourages user engagement and interaction. The device's modern design and user-friendly features may create a sense of trust and reliability despite the underlying complexity of its algorithms and decision-making processes.

In summary, while the Nest Learning Thermostat prioritizes user welfare by offering energy-saving benefits and convenience, its design involves elements of psychological manipulation that may not fully align with the principle of honesty in design.

E-Commerce Sites

E-commerce sites often leverage persuasive techniques to influence user behaviour and encourage desired actions such as making a purchase, signing up for newsletters, or engaging with content. These techniques draw from principles of psychology and marketing to create a more compelling and engaging user experience. While some critics may view these techniques as manipulative, they are often employed with the intention of enhancing the user experience and providing value to customers.

Here are some common persuasive techniques used in e-commerce sites and why they are utilized for the benefit of customers:

1. **Social Proof**: E-commerce sites often feature user reviews, ratings, and testimonials to provide social proof of the product's quality and popularity. When customers see positive feedback from other users, they are more likely to trust the product and feel confident in their purchasing decisions. Social proof helps alleviate concerns and uncertainties, making the shopping experience more reassuring for customers.

2. **Scarcity and Urgency**: Many e-commerce sites use tactics such as limited-time offers, countdown timers, and low-stock alerts to create a sense of urgency and scarcity. By highlighting the limited availability of products or time-sensitive deals, e-commerce sites motivate customers to make a purchase sooner rather than later. While these techniques may prompt impulse buying, they also ensure that customers have access to

exclusive discounts or products before they run out.

3. **Personalization**: E-commerce sites leverage data analytics and user profiling to personalize the shopping experience for each customer. Through techniques such as product recommendations, tailored promotions, and customized content, e-commerce sites cater to the unique preferences and interests of individual users. Personalization enhances user engagement, increases relevance, and streamlines the decision-making process for customers, ultimately leading to a more satisfying shopping experience.

4. **Visual Cues and Design**: The layout, colour scheme, and visual elements of an e-commerce site play a crucial role in shaping user behaviour and perception. Eye-catching banners, call-to-action buttons, and product images are strategically placed to guide users through the shopping journey and draw attention to key features or promotions. Clear navigation menus and intuitive search functions ensure that customers can easily find what they are looking for, reducing frustration and enhancing usability.

5. **Incentives and Rewards**: E-commerce sites often offer incentives such as discounts, free shipping, loyalty points, or exclusive access to premium content to incentivize customer engagement and repeat purchases. These rewards serve as motivators for customers to explore the site, interact with promotional offers, and remain loyal to the brand. By providing tangible benefits to customers, e-commerce sites foster a sense of value and appreciation, encouraging long-term relationships and brand advocacy.

While e-commerce sites employ persuasive techniques to influence user behaviour, they do so with the aim of enhancing the user experience and delivering value to customers. By leveraging psychological principles and data-driven insights, e-commerce sites create more engaging, relevant, and personalized interactions that meet the diverse needs and preferences of modern consumers.

In these cases, designers carefully balance the use of persuasive techniques with ethical considerations, ensuring that users are not deceived or manipulated. The goal is to engage users and encourage certain behaviours while still maintaining a level of transparency and integrity.

UX/UI

An example from UX/UI where the principle of "Good Design is Honest" may be challenged is in the design of progress indicators or loading animations.

When users interact with digital platforms or applications, they often encounter loading screens or progress indicators that provide feedback on the system's processing status. While the primary purpose of these elements is to manage user expectations and communicate progress, designers may sometimes employ techniques that manipulate the perception of time or progress.

For instance, a progress indicator may show continuous motion or animation, giving users the impression that something is happening in the background. However, behind the scenes, the actual progress may be slower or involve several sequential steps. This design approach is known as a "fake progress bar." It creates a perception of progress, even if the process itself is not advancing at the same rate.

While this technique can help alleviate user frustration and create a more engaging experience, it deviates from complete transparency. It manipulates the perception of time and progress to enhance user satisfaction. However, in terms of strict honesty, it does not provide an accurate representation of the actual processing time.

Another example is in the design of confirmation messages or success notifications. Designers may use positive language, vivid visuals, or celebratory animations to convey a sense of accomplishment or success to users. While these design choices can enhance the user experience and create positive emotions, they may not always reflect the true significance or impact of the user's action.

In both cases, designers are employing techniques that balance transparency and user experience. While the design may not be completely transparent or honest in terms of representing the actual processes or outcomes, it serves the purpose of managing user expectations, reducing frustration, and enhancing engagement.

Endowment Effect

Designers sometimes employ strategies that could be perceived as dishonest to encourage users to invest in a product or service, understanding that the endowment effect can play a significant role in enhancing the user experience. The endowment effect suggests that individuals tend to attribute more value to something they have invested in, both emotionally and cognitively.

For example, social media platforms often encourage users to complete their profiles by providing personal information and uploading photos. While this may initially seem like an invasion of privacy or a potentially dishonest request, it is designed to personalize the user's experience and build a sense of ownership. By investing their time and personal data, users begin to feel a stronger connection to the platform. This sense of ownership and investment motivates users to engage more actively, connect with others, and derive greater value from the platform.

Similarly, online productivity tools or task management applications may request users to invest time in setting up their accounts, organizing tasks, or learning how to use advanced features. While this may require an upfront effort from the users, it is designed to optimize their productivity in the long run. By investing their time and effort into mastering the tool, users can experience the full range of features, streamline their workflows, and ultimately benefit from increased efficiency and effectiveness.

Endowment Effect Through Effort: The concept of "Endowment through Effort" refers to the psychological phenomenon where individuals attribute greater value to something they have invested time, energy, or effort into creating or acquiring. This cognitive bias influences decision-making processes and can lead individuals to place a higher perceived value on items or experiences that they have actively contributed to or customized. Endowment through effort plays a significant role in consumer behavior, product satisfaction, and brand loyalty, highlighting the importance of user engagement and involvement in shaping perceptions of value and ownership.

An example of a product that leverages the concept of Endowment through Effort is the IKEA furniture assembly experience. When customers purchase furniture from IKEA, they often need to assemble it themselves using the provided instructions and tools. While this DIY approach may initially seem daunting or time-consuming, it actually fosters a sense of ownership and attachment to the furniture.

Customers who invest time and effort into assembling their IKEA furniture perceive it as more valuable because of the personal involvement in its creation. Even though the process may be challenging at times and require problem-solving skills, customers often feel a sense of accomplishment and pride once the furniture is successfully assembled.

Despite the perception that IKEA could simply provide pre-assembled furniture for convenience, the DIY assembly model aligns with the principle of Endowment through Effort. By engaging customers in the assembly process, IKEA enhances the perceived value of its products and fosters a deeper connection with its brand.

In these cases, designers strategically employ persuasive techniques to nudge users towards investing in the product or service. While this approach may be considered somewhat deceptive, it is ultimately aimed at enhancing the user experience and providing long-term value. By leveraging the endowment effect and encouraging users to become active participants in the product, designers can foster a stronger sense of engagement, satisfaction, and enjoyment.

Choice Paradox

The choice paradox refers to the phenomenon where offering too many options or overwhelming users with excessive information can lead to decision-making difficulties and a reduced overall product experience. As a result, designers often find themselves in a position where they need to hide or reduce certain visible features in order to alleviate cognitive load and assist users in making more informed decisions.

For instance, consider an e-commerce website that offers a wide range of products in a specific category. If all the available options were presented to users simultaneously, it could lead to decision fatigue and frustration. The abundance of choices may create an overwhelming experience, making it difficult for users to make a confident and satisfactory decision. In such a scenario, designers might employ strategies like categorizing products, utilizing filters, or employing recommendation algorithms to narrow down the selection and simplify the decision-making process. By presenting users with a more curated and manageable set of options, the design aims to enhance the user experience and alleviate the cognitive burden associated with excessive choices.

Another example can be seen in the design of mobile applications. App developers often face the challenge of balancing functionality and simplicity. Including too many visible features or overwhelming users with complex navigation can hinder usability and diminish the overall user experience. To address this, designers may adopt a minimalist approach by simplifying the interface, hiding certain features behind menus or submenus, or utilizing progressive disclosure techniques. By reducing the visible complexity and providing a more streamlined interface, designers aim to enhance usability, reduce cognitive load, and guide users towards the most relevant and useful features.

In these examples, designers prioritize the user's experience by selectively hiding or reducing certain visible features. While this approach may deviate from complete transparency, it serves the purpose of improving usability and decision-making.

In conclusion, the principle of "Good Design is Honest" serves as a foundational tenet in design philosophy, emphasizing transparency, integrity, and sincerity in the creation of products and experiences. However, its practical application is complex and multifaceted, often challenging designers to navigate ethical dilemmas, cultural nuances, and user perceptions while balancing business objectives and user welfare.

Critiques of the principle highlight the subjective nature of truthfulness, the influence of marketing tactics on honesty, and the complexities of user perception versus reality. Designers must grapple with issues such as complexity, omission, and regulatory constraints while striving to maintain integrity and transparency in their designs.

Moreover, the use of psychological principles and persuasive techniques, such as the Peak-End Rule, gamification, and the endowment effect, may sometimes deviate from strict notions of honesty but are employed with the intention of enhancing user experience and welfare.

Ultimately, designers must carefully consider the implications of their design choices, balancing honesty with other design objectives while prioritizing the interests and experiences of users. By managing user expectations, providing a positive experience, and ensuring ethical practices, designers can build trust, loyalty, and satisfaction among users, fostering meaningful and impactful design outcomes.

* * *

06 -Good Design is Long Lasting

Dieter Rams' principle of "Good Design is Long Lasting" emphasizes the importance of durability, timelessness, and sustainability in design.

Durability: Good design should be durable, meaning it is built to last over time. Products should be constructed from high-quality materials and manufactured with precision to withstand wear and tear, usage, and environmental factors. Durability ensures that products maintain their functionality, structural integrity, and aesthetic appeal throughout their lifespan, reducing the need for frequent repairs or replacements.

Timelessness: Good design transcends trends and fads, possessing a timeless quality that remains relevant and appealing across generations. Timeless designs eschew gimmicks, flashy embellishments, or excessive ornamentation in favor of clean, simple forms and universal aesthetics. By avoiding elements that quickly become outdated, timeless designs retain their relevance and appeal over the long term, enduring changes in taste and style.

Functionality: Long-lasting design prioritizes functionality and utility, ensuring that products serve their intended purpose effectively and efficiently. Designers should focus on user needs, ergonomics, and usability, creating products that enhance the user experience and address practical concerns. Functional design elements should be intuitive, reliable, and easy to use, contributing to the overall longevity and value of the product.

Repairability and Upgradability: Good design facilitates repair, maintenance, and upgrades, allowing products to be serviced and refurbished rather than discarded when issues arise or new features are desired. Designers should consider modularity, accessibility of components, and compatibility with future technologies to enable easy repairs and upgrades. Repairable and upgradable products promote sustainability by extending their lifespan and reducing waste.

Sustainability: Long-lasting design embraces principles of environmental sustainability, minimizing resource consumption, pollution, and ecological impact throughout the product lifecycle. Sustainable design practices include using recyclable materials, reducing energy consumption during manufacturing and use, minimizing packaging waste, and designing for disassembly and recycling at the end of the product's life. By adopting sustainable design principles, designers can create products that contribute to a more environmentally conscious and responsible society.

In summary, Dieter Rams' principle of "Good Design is Long Lasting" underscores the importance of durability, timelessness, functionality, repairability, upgradability, and sustainability in design. Long-lasting design not only enhances the user experience and adds value to products but also promotes responsible consumption, environmental stewardship, and social consciousness.

The Critique

Here are some critiques of this principle:

1. **Changing Trends and Tastes**: One challenge with designing products to be long-lasting is that consumer tastes and trends are constantly evolving. What may be considered timeless and durable today may become outdated or less desirable in the future. Designers may struggle to predict and anticipate shifting preferences, making it difficult to create truly long-lasting designs that remain relevant over extended periods.
2. **Technological Obsolescence**: In today's fast-paced technological landscape, products can become obsolete relatively quickly due to advancements in technology and innovation. Designing products to be long-

lasting may be challenging when rapid technological developments render existing features or functionalities obsolete. Consumers may prioritize the latest technologies over durability and longevity, leading to shorter product lifecycles and reduced emphasis on long-lasting design.

3. **Planned Obsolescence**: Some critics argue that planned obsolescence, where products are deliberately designed to have a limited lifespan or become obsolete after a certain period, undermines the principle of long-lasting design. Companies may intentionally incorporate design elements or manufacturing practices that encourage consumers to replace products more frequently, thereby stimulating demand and driving sales. Planned obsolescence can conflict with sustainability goals and consumer interests by promoting wasteful consumption and disposable culture.

4. **Environmental Impact**: While long-lasting design principles emphasize sustainability and environmental responsibility, the manufacturing processes and materials used in product design can still have significant environmental impacts. Extracting raw materials, energy-intensive manufacturing processes, and disposal of end-of-life products con-tribute to resource depletion, pollution, and environmental degradation. Designers must consider the full lifecycle of products and prioritize sus-tainable materials, production methods, and end-of-life considerations to mitigate environmental harm.

5. **Cost Considerations**: Designing products to be long-lasting may entail higher upfront costs due to investments in quality materials, precision manufacturing, and durability testing. Consumers may be unwilling to pay premium prices for products perceived as long-lasting, especially if they prioritize affordability or short-term convenience over durability and sustainability. Balancing cost considerations with the principles of long-lasting design can be challenging for designers and companies seeking to appeal to price-sensitive consumers.

6. **Cultural and Societal Shifts**: Long-lasting design principles may not always align with cultural or societal values, particularly in consumer-driven societies where novelty, trendiness, and disposability are often

prized. Societal norms and lifestyle preferences can influence consumer behaviour and perceptions of value, impacting the adoption of long-lasting design practices. Designers must navigate cultural nuances and consumer expectations to create products that resonate with diverse audiences while promoting longevity and sustainability.

7. **Regulatory and Legal Constraints**: Regulatory frameworks and legal requirements may impose limitations on the design, production, and marketing of products, affecting the feasibility of long-lasting design principles. Intellectual property laws, safety standards, environmental regulations, and product liability considerations can influence design decisions and add complexity to the development process. Designers must ensure compliance with applicable laws and regulations while striving to integrate long-lasting design principles into their products.

8. **Consumer Preferences and Behaviors:** Ultimately, the success of the long-lasting design depends on consumer preferences, behaviours, and perceptions of value. While some consumers may prioritize durability, sustainability, and longevity in their purchasing decisions, others may prioritize features, aesthetics, or affordability. Designers must understand and adapt to diverse consumer preferences while advocating for the benefits of long-lasting design and educating consumers about the importance of sustainability and responsible consumption.

While the principle that "Good Design is Long Lasting" emphasizes durability, timelessness, functionality, repairability, upgradability, and sustainability, its practical application is complex and multifaceted. Designers must navigate evolving trends, technological advancements, consumer preferences, regulatory requirements, and environmental considerations to create products that balance longevity, sustainability, and user satisfaction. Despite its challenges and limitations, long-lasting design remains an aspirational goal for designers committed to promoting responsible consumption, environmental stewardship, and social well-being.

Nokia

An example that challenges the principle of "Good Design is Long Lasting" due to changing consumer trends and tastes is Nokia. Nokia was once a dominant force in the mobile phone industry, known for producing durable and reliable handsets with iconic designs.

In the early 2000s, Nokia's candy bar-style phones, such as the Nokia 3310, were highly popular due to their robust build quality, long battery life, and simple user interface. These phones were considered timeless and durable, embodying the principles of long-lasting design.

However, as consumer preferences and technological advancements evolved, Nokia struggled to adapt to changing trends in the mobile phone market. The emergence of smartphones with touchscreens, app ecosystems, and advanced multimedia capabilities shifted consumer expectations towards more feature-rich and customizable devices.

Nokia's reluctance to embrace touchscreen technology and its adherence to traditional phone designs led to a decline in market share and relevance. Competitors like Apple's iPhone and Samsung's Galaxy series captured consumer interest with innovative features, sleek designs, and intuitive user experiences, challenging Nokia's position as a market leader.

Despite Nokia's legacy of producing durable and reliable phones, its failure to anticipate and respond to changing trends ultimately undermined the principle of long-lasting design.

BlackBerry

BlackBerry, formerly known as Research In Motion (RIM), was once a dominant player in the smartphone market, particularly in the business and enterprise segments. BlackBerry devices were renowned for their physical QWERTY keyboards, secure messaging capabilities, and robust email integration, making them popular among professionals and corporate users.

During the early 2000s and the first half of the 2010s, BlackBerry enjoyed considerable success and market dominance, with its devices considered reliable, efficient, and synonymous with productivity. The brand's iconic design, characterized by the distinctive keyboard layout and BlackBerry Messenger (BBM) service, contributed to its reputation for delivering long-lasting and functional smartphones.

However, as consumer preferences shifted towards touchscreen devices and app-centric ecosystems, BlackBerry struggled to adapt its product offerings to meet evolving market demands. The rise of touchscreen smartphones, led by Apple's iPhone and later Android devices, revolutionized the mobile industry and redefined user expectations regarding usability, functionality, and design aesthetics.

BlackBerry's insistence on maintaining its signature physical keyboards and focus on enterprise-oriented features limited its appeal to mainstream consumers, who increasingly favoured touchscreen interfaces, multimedia capabilities, and access to a wide range of third-party apps.

The company's delayed response to changing market trends, coupled with a lack of innovation in hardware and software, contributed to a decline in BlackBerry's market share and relevance. Despite attempts to launch touchscreen devices and modernize its operating system with BlackBerry 10, the brand struggled to regain momentum and faced stiff competition from rival platforms.

In summary, BlackBerry's experience serves as a cautionary tale about the challenges of maintaining long-lasting design in an ever-evolving market-place.

GoPro

GoPro revolutionized the action camera market with its compact, rugged cameras designed to capture high-quality footage in extreme conditions. The brand gained widespread popularity among outdoor enthusiasts, athletes, and adventurers seeking to document their experiences with hands-free, wearable cameras.

However, despite its initial success, GoPro faced significant challenges related to technological obsolescence. The rapid pace of innovation in the consumer electronics industry led to frequent upgrades in camera technology, including improvements in resolution, image stabilization, and connectivity features.

As a result, GoPro's product lineup became susceptible to technological obsolescence, with newer camera models boasting superior performance and advanced features compared to their predecessors. Consumers, particularly early adopters and tech enthusiasts, increasingly gravitated towards the latest GoPro models, leaving older generations of cameras outdated and less desirable.

GoPro's product strategy, which emphasized incremental upgrades and frequent product releases to stay competitive in the market, posed challenges for the longevity and long-term viability of its devices. While each new camera iteration introduced enhancements and refinements, it also accelerated the pace at which older models became obsolete, limiting their lifespan and resale value.

Additionally, GoPro's reliance on proprietary accessories and ecosystem lock-in further compounded the issue of technological obsolescence. Changes in connector types, mounting systems, and compatibility requirements made it difficult for users to extend the lifespan of their cameras or integrate them with third-party accessories and peripherals.

Despite efforts to innovate and diversify its product offerings, GoPro's struggle to address the issue of technological obsolescence impacted its brand reputation and financial performance. The company faced challenges related to declining sales, excess inventory, and heightened competition from rival manufacturers offering comparable action cameras at lower price points.

In response, GoPro shifted its focus towards software and subscription-based services, such as GoPro Plus and GoPro Labs, to enhance user engagement and generate recurring revenue streams. However, the underlying issue of technological obsolescence remained a persistent challenge for the brand as it sought to balance innovation with the longevity of its products.

Overall, GoPro's experience underscores the complexities of designing products for long-lasting durability in an industry characterized by rapid technological advancements and changing consumer preferences. The brand's efforts to navigate the tension between innovation and obsolescence highlight the inherent trade-offs involved in achieving sustainable design and product longevity in the digital age.

Aesthetics

The principle of "Good design is long-lasting" can indeed be challenged when it comes to the aesthetics of a product. People's tastes and preferences are constantly evolving, and what may be considered stylish and trendy today may quickly become outdated in the future. This rapid shift in fashion and design trends poses a challenge to the idea of long-lasting design.

One of the reasons for the short lifespan of certain design styles is the influence of popular culture and the media. Trends are often driven by celebrities, influencers, and the constant bombardment of new styles through various media channels. These influences can lead to a rapid turnover in aesthetic preferences, with people seeking the latest and most fashionable designs.

Another factor that contributes to the shorter lifespan of design styles is the rise of fast fashion and consumerism. With the availability of affordable and easily accessible fashion and design products, consumers are more inclined to change their preferences frequently and follow the latest trends. This constant demand for new and updated styles puts pressure on designers and manufacturers to keep up with the changing market, resulting in shorter product lifecycles.

Additionally, advancements in technology and manufacturing processes have made it easier and more cost-effective to produce and distribute new designs quickly. This acceleration in the design and production cycles further contributes to the shorter lifespan of aesthetics in products.

In conclusion, while the principle of "Good Design is Long Lasting" emphasizes durability and sustainability, its practical application faces challenges stemming from changing trends, technological obsolescence, and consumer preferences. Designers must navigate these complexities to create products that balance longevity with innovation and relevance in evolving markets.

* * *

07 -Good Design is Thorough Down to the Last Detail

D ieter Rams' principle of "Good Design is Thorough Down to the Last Detail" emphasizes the importance of meticulous attention to every aspect of a design, from its overall concept to the smallest details. This principle underscores the notion that excellence in design requires careful consideration of all elements, ensuring cohesiveness, functionality, and aesthetic harmony throughout the product.

Rams believed that every component of a design should serve a purpose and contribute to the overall user experience. From the layout of buttons to the choice of materials, each detail should be thoughtfully crafted to enhance usability, durability, and visual appeal. By paying attention to the finer points of design, designers can create products that are intuitive, elegant, and timeless.

Furthermore, Rams' principle highlights the significance of consistency and coherence in design language. A cohesive design language ensures that all elements of a product, whether visible or hidden, align with its overarching concept and brand identity. Consistency in design fosters familiarity, usability, and brand recognition, strengthening the relationship between the product and its users.

In essence, "Good Design is Thorough Down to the Last Detail" empha-sizes the meticulous craftsmanship, thoughtful consideration, and holistic approach required to achieve excellence in design. It serves as a guiding principle for designers seeking to create products that are not only functional and beautiful but also enduring and meaningful in their execution.

The Critique

Like any principle, this one also has some limitations:

1. **Feasibility and Practicality**: One critique of this principle is that achieving thoroughness down to the last detail may not always be feasible or practical, especially in complex design projects with tight timelines or budget constraints. Designers may face limitations in terms of resources, time, or technical capabilities, making it challenging to devote extensive attention to every detail without compromising other aspects of the design process.

2. **Over-Engineering**: In some cases, striving for thoroughness down to the last detail may lead to over-engineering or unnecessary complexity in design. Designers may become overly focused on perfecting minor details or features that have minimal impact on the overall user experience. This excessive attention to detail can result in bloated designs, increased production costs, and diminished user satisfaction.

3. **Diminished Creativity**: The pursuit of thoroughness in design may stifle creativity and innovation by imposing rigid standards or criteria for every detail. Designers may feel constrained by the need to adhere strictly to predefined guidelines or specifications, limiting their ability to explore unconventional ideas or push the boundaries of design innovation. This can lead to formulaic or uninspired designs that lack originality and fail to captivate users.

4. **Subjectivity in Detailing**: Another critique is the subjective nature of detailing in design. What may be considered thorough and meticulous to one designer or stakeholder may not necessarily resonate with users or meet their expectations. Designers must navigate diverse perspectives, preferences, and cultural contexts when determining which details are essential and how they should be executed, highlighting the inherent

subjectivity in design decision-making.

5. **Risk of Micromanagement**: The principle of thoroughness down to the last detail may inadvertently promote micromanagement within design teams or organizations. Managers or stakeholders may exert undue pressure on designers to scrutinize every aspect of a design, leading to micromanagement, burnout, and diminished morale among team members. This can hinder collaboration, creativity, and the free exchange of ideas within the design process.

6. **Trade-offs and Prioritization**: Designers often face trade-offs and prioritization challenges when striving for thoroughness in design. They must balance competing demands such as functionality, aesthetics, usability, and manufacturability while ensuring that every detail contributes meaningfully to the overall user experience. This requires careful decision-making and trade-off analysis to allocate resources effectively and optimize the design outcome.

7. **Resource Intensiveness**: Achieving thoroughness down to the last detail may require significant investment of time, effort, and resources, particularly in terms of research, prototyping, and iteration. Designers must allocate sufficient resources and allocate priorities to different aspects of the design process, recognizing that thoroughness in one area may come at the expense of others.

8. **Risk of Perfectionism**: The pursuit of thoroughness down to the last detail may lead to perfectionism within design teams, where designers strive for unattainable standards of perfection in every aspect of the design. This perfectionist mindset can create unrealistic expectations, increase stress and anxiety among team members, and ultimately impede progress and innovation in the design process.

9. **Diminished Iteration and Adaptation**: Focusing too much on perfecting every detail from the outset may discourage designers from embracing iteration, experimentation, and adaptation in the design process. Design is inherently iterative, requiring constant refinement and adjustment based on user feedback, market trends, and technological advancements. Overemphasis on thoroughness in the initial design phase may hinder

designers' ability to iterate and adapt their designs in response to evolving needs and circumstances.

10. **Impact on Time-to-Market**: The pursuit of thoroughness down to the last detail may prolong the design process and delay time-to-market for products or services. Designers may invest significant time and effort in perfecting minor details or refining aesthetic elements, leading to delays in product development and commercialization. In fast-paced industries or competitive markets, excessive attention to detail may result in missed opportunities and reduced market share for organizations.

11. **Diminishing Returns:** There comes a point where the effort invested in perfecting every small detail yields diminishing returns in terms of user experience or overall value. While attention to detail is essential, it is important to prioritize and allocate resources effectively to focus on the aspects that have the most significant impact on the user's experience.

12. **Context and Purpose:** The level of detail required may vary depending on the context and purpose of the product. For example, a highly detailed design may be necessary for certain industries such as luxury goods, where aesthetics and craftsmanship are paramount. However, for products that prioritize functionality or efficiency, excessive attention to detail may not be as crucial.

13. **Cost:** In many cases, meticulously addressing every detail can result in an increase in design, prototyping, and manufacturing costs, which may ultimately impact the final price of the product. If the price becomes too high, it may deter potential buyers and limit the product's market appeal. Therefore, designers and manufacturers often need to strike a balance between addressing essential details and managing costs to ensure the product remains competitive and accessible to consumers. Furthermore, not all details have the same impact on the user experience or functionality of the product. Some aspects may be more crucial than others, and it is essential to prioritize those aspects that have the greatest influence on the product's success. This means that certain details may need to be compromised or simplified to maintain a reasonable price point without significantly sacrificing usability or performance.

By carefully selecting which details to focus on and compromising on less critical aspects, designers can create products that meet consumer needs while managing production costs. This approach ensures that the product remains attractive to the target market without burdening consumers with unnecessary expenses.

While the principle "Good Design is Thorough Down to the Last Detail" underscores the importance of meticulous attention and craftsmanship in design, designers must be mindful of its potential pitfalls and challenges. By embracing flexibility, iteration, and user-centricity, designers can achieve excellence in design while navigating the complexities of the design process effectively.

IKEA

IKEA is renowned for its affordable and functional furniture designs, which often prioritize simplicity and mass production over meticulous detailing. While IKEA products are well-designed in terms of functionality and affordability, they may not always exhibit the level of thoroughness in craftsmanship and detail that some other high-end furniture brands prioritize.

For instance, IKEA furniture pieces often feature assembly instructions that focus on simplicity and ease of construction, sometimes at the expense of intricate detailing or luxurious finishes. While this approach allows IKEA to produce cost-effective furniture that appeals to a wide audience, it may not align with the meticulous attention to detail emphasized by the principle.

Additionally, IKEA's flat-pack furniture design, while innovative and space-efficient, may lack the intricate craftsmanship and bespoke detailing found in artisanal furniture pieces. The emphasis on scalability, affordability, and ease of transportation often takes precedence over the meticulous detailing that characterizes luxury furniture brands.

Despite these considerations, IKEA's design philosophy aligns with its mission of providing accessible and functional home furnishing solutions to the masses. While the brand may not adhere strictly to the principle of thoroughness down to the last detail, its focus on simplicity, affordability, and practicality resonates with millions of customers worldwide.

Budget Friendly Entry-level Cars

Budget-friendly cars are known for their affordability, simplicity, and reliability. They were designed to meet the basic transportation needs of customers who prioritize value for money over luxury features. To keep costs low and make the car accessible to a wider audience, the manufacturer may have made compromises in specific areas:

Styling and Aesthetics: The design of those cars is generally straightforward and practical, focusing more on functionality rather than cutting-edge aesthetics. The exterior styling may be simple and lack some of the sleek and sporty elements seen in higher-end cars. However, this approach allows for easier manufacturing and cost savings.

Fit and Finish: The fit and finish of the cars' interiors were not as refined as in more expensive cars. There might have been some inconsistencies in panel gaps or alignment, and the overall attention to detail in terms of finishing touches might have been lacking. However, these compromises were made to reduce production costs and offer an affordable car to the mass market.

For example — The design and construction of the wiper water lid might be simpler and less robust compared to luxury cars. It may not have a soft-close mechanism or a high-quality latch system. Instead, it could be a basic plastic cap that serves its purpose of protecting the wiper water reservoir.

The door handles may have a more utilitarian design, prioritizing functionality over sophisticated aesthetics and texture. While they may be ergonomically designed for easy gripping and pulling, they might lack the smooth, polished and rigid feel found in luxury cars.

When designing seats for low-end cars, manufacturers often prioritize functionality and affordability over luxurious comfort. While seats in these vehicles may still serve their primary purpose of providing a place to sit, they may not offer the same level of ergonomic support or customization options as higher-end counterparts.

For instance, the seat padding and cushioning in low-end cars may be thinner or less plush compared to those in more expensive models. The seat profiles may lack the contouring and adjustable features found in ergonomic seats, limiting the level of personalized comfort that can be achieved.

These compromises in seat design are made to maintain affordability and ensure that the cost of the vehicle remains accessible to a broader market segment. While this may result in a trade-off in terms of long-term comfort and ergonomics, it allows manufacturers to offer budget-friendly options that fulfil basic seating requirements.

Motorola Moto G

The Motorola Moto G series is known for offering affordable smartphones with decent performance and essential features at a competitive price point. While the Moto G phones may not boast the same level of premium materials or advanced technology as flagship smartphones from other brands, they excel in providing a reliable and functional user experience.

Here's how the Moto G series demonstrates success despite not delving into intricate details:

1. **Build Quality and Materials:** The Moto G phones typically feature a plastic build with a simple and utilitarian design. While they may not have the sleek metal or glass construction seen in higher-end smartphones, the plastic build helps keep production costs low without compromising durability.
2. **Display and Aesthetics:** The display panels used in Moto G phones may not have the highest resolution or pixel density compared to flagship devices. However, they still offer vibrant colors and sufficient brightness for everyday use. The design of the phone is functional rather than flashy, focusing on ergonomic considerations and ease of use.

3. **Camera Performance:** While the camera systems on Moto G phones may not rival those found in premium smartphones, they still deliver decent image quality for everyday photography. The cameras lack some of the advanced features and image processing capabilities found in flagship devices but are more than adequate for capturing memorable moments and sharing photos on social media.

4. **Software and Performance:** Moto G phones run on near-stock Android software with minimal bloatware and customizations. While they may not offer the same level of software optimization or exclusive features as flagship devices, they provide a clean and responsive user experience. The hardware specifications are tailored to deliver smooth performance for everyday tasks such as web browsing, social media, and multimedia consumption.

5. **Battery Life and Connectivity:** Moto G phones prioritize battery life and connectivity, offering all-day battery performance and support for essential connectivity features such as 4G LTE and Wi-Fi. While they may not support the latest wireless charging or high-speed data technologies, they still deliver reliable connectivity for staying connected on the go.

Overall, the success of the Motorola Moto G series lies in its ability to deliver a solid smartphone experience at an accessible price point. Despite not delving into intricate details or offering the latest cutting-edge features, Moto G phones cater to the needs of budget-conscious consumers who value reliability, affordability, and functional design.

McDonald's

McDonald's is known for its efficient, standardized food production processes and quick service. While the company pays attention to detail in various aspects of its operations, there are limits to how much detail can be perfected without significantly increasing costs or slowing down service.

For example, consider the design of McDonald's packaging. McDonald's invests in designing packaging that is functional, visually appealing, and promotes brand recognition. The packaging is carefully crafted to hold food securely, maintain freshness, and facilitate convenient consumption, whether dining in or taking out.

While the company strives for optimal packaging design, there are limits to how much detail can be refined without significantly increasing costs or disrupting the speed of service.

For instance, the process of packaging food by staff may be optimized to shave off a few seconds, but such gains must be balanced against potential cost increases and the primary consumer need for affordability. While shorter wait times are desirable, beyond a certain point, the value gained may not outweigh the added expenses.

In addressing the usability of packaging, McDonald's faces challenges such as keeping burgers secure without excessive movement, all while minimizing inventory complexity and handling costs. Thus, the company may compromise on certain packaging details to maintain efficient delivery and affordability, which are critical value propositions for customers.

Cost considerations also influence the selection of packaging materials and structural designs. While self-sealing options or intricate structural features may enhance the user experience, they could significantly raise production costs. McDonald's prioritizes functionality over intricate detailing to ensure that packaging meets basic requirements at the lowest feasible cost.

Additionally, the disposal of take-out packaging after use is an important aspect to consider. While environmental sustainability is increasingly important, the brand must balance this concern with the overall cost and feasibility of implementing eco-friendly solutions.

By focusing on the most impactful aspects of packaging design while balancing cost considerations, McDonald's effectively manages the law of diminishing returns in attention to detail. The company recognizes that excessive detailing beyond a certain point may not significantly improve customer satisfaction or loyalty, especially in a fast-paced, cost-conscious industry like fast food.

In conclusion, while Dieter Rams' principle of "Good Design is Thorough Down to the Last Detail" emphasizes meticulous attention to every aspect of design, it also presents challenges such as feasibility constraints, over-engineering risks, and the subjective nature of detailing. Designers must balance thoroughness with practicality, creativity, and resource efficiency to create impactful and user-centric designs that resonate with their audience.

* * *

08 -Good Design is Unobtrusive

D ieter Rams' principle of "Good Design is Unobtrusive" emphasizes the idea that well-designed products should not impose themselves on users or draw unnecessary attention to their presence. Instead, they should seamlessly integrate into users' lives, environments, and activities without causing distractions or disruptions. This principle underscores the importance of simplicity, clarity, and user-centeredness in design, where the focus is on enhancing usability, functionality, and overall user experience while minimizing unnecessary complexity or visual clutter.

In essence, "Good Design is Unobtrusive" suggests that products should serve their intended purpose efficiently and intuitively, without overshadowing or intruding upon the user's primary tasks or objectives. This principle aligns with Rams' broader philosophy of minimalist design, which advocates for clarity, restraint, and elegance in form and function. By prioritizing simplicity and subtlety, designers can create products that feel natural, intuitive, and harmonious in their interactions with users.

Rams believed that truly effective design should be felt rather than seen, with the product's presence fading into the background as users engage with it effortlessly and seamlessly. This requires careful attention to detail, thoughtful consideration of user needs and preferences, and a commitment to stripping away unnecessary elements or embellishments that detract from the product's core functionality or purpose.

In summary, "Good Design is Unobtrusive" encourages designers to create products that blend seamlessly into users' lives, environments, and activities. Now, let's proceed with the critique of this principle.

The Critique

1. **Subjectivity of Perception:** One of the primary challenges with the principle of unobtrusive design is the subjective nature of what constitutes obtrusiveness. What may be perceived as unobtrusive by one user or cultural context may not necessarily be the same for another. While minimalism can create a clean and uncluttered design, it may also result in a lack of visual interest or fail to evoke emotional responses in users. Designers must navigate diverse perspectives and preferences when determining the appropriate level of visibility or subtlety for a product.

2. **Balancing Visibility and Functionality:** While striving for unobtrusive design, there is a risk of sacrificing the visibility and discoverability of important features or functions. Designers must strike a delicate balance between making essential elements readily accessible to users and minimizing visual clutter or distractions. Overemphasis on unobtrusiveness may lead to hidden functionalities or confusing user interfaces, hindering usability and learnability.

3. **User Experience:** One of the main criticisms of this principle is that it can lead to oversimplification, resulting in inadequate user experience. By striving to remove as much design as possible, designers may inadvertently eliminate essential features or compromise usability. Users rely on certain design elements to navigate and interact with products effectively. Removing those elements in the pursuit of minimalism can hinder usability and frustrate users.

4. **Emotional Connection:** An unobtrusive design can sometimes result in a lack of user engagement or emotional connection. If a product is too discreet or unassuming, it may fail to evoke excitement or enthusiasm in users. Some consumers appreciate products that make a bold statement, reflect their personality, or evoke a sense of delight. By prioritizing unobtrusiveness, designers may overlook opportunities to create memorable and emotionally engaging experiences.

5. **Innovation and Differentiation:** One potential criticism of unobtrusiveness is that it can sometimes lead to a lack of innovation or differentiation.

When a product is designed to blend in and not stand out, it may become indistinguishable from similar products in the market. This can hinder a brand's ability to create a unique identity or capture consumer attention. In competitive industries where product differentiation is crucial, being unobtrusive may result in a lack of market impact.

6. **Contextual Considerations:** The appropriateness of unobtrusive design depends heavily on the context in which the product is used. In certain environments or applications, such as safety-critical systems or emergency situations, visibility and prominence of design elements are paramount. Designers must consider the specific needs, constraints, and user expectations within each context to determine the optimal level of obtrusiveness for a given design.

7. **Brand Identity and Expression:** While unobtrusive design aligns well with minimalist aesthetics and user-centric principles, it may not always reflect the brand identity or expression desired by organizations. Some brands may intentionally seek to make a bold statement or create memorable experiences through distinctive design elements that stand out and capture users' attention. Designers must balance the principles of unobtrusiveness with the strategic objectives and brand values of their clients or organizations.

8. **Accessibility and Inclusivity:** In striving for unobtrusive design, there is a risk of overlooking the needs of users with diverse abilities or preferences. Certain users may rely on clear visual cues, auditory feedback, or tactile indicators to interact effectively with products and interfaces. Designers must ensure that unobtrusive design principles do not inadvertently exclude or marginalize users with disabilities or special requirements.

9. **Technological Constraints:** The feasibility of implementing unobtrusive design principles may be limited by technological constraints or platform-specific considerations. Certain design elements or interaction patterns may be difficult to achieve without compromising performance, compatibility, or security. Designers must work within the constraints of available technologies and platforms while striving to create unobtrusive

and user-friendly experiences.

10. **Evolving User Expectations:** User expectations and design trends are constantly evolving, influencing perceptions of what constitutes unobtrusive design. As new technologies emerge and user behaviours evolve, designers must adapt their approaches to accommodate changing preferences and expectations. What may be considered unobtrusive today may not necessarily hold true in the future, requiring designers to remain flexible and responsive to emerging trends and user needs.

11. **Psychological Impact:** Unobtrusive design aims to minimize cognitive load and distractions for users, promoting a seamless and intuitive user experience. However, there are instances where subtle design elements can have a profound psychological impact on user perception and behaviour. Designers must be mindful of how visual hierarchy, colour psychology, and micro-interactions influence user engagement and emotional response.

12. **Long-Term Impact:** While unobtrusive design aims to create seamless and frictionless user experiences, its long-term impact on user behaviour and well-being requires careful consideration. Excessive streamlining and automation of tasks may diminish users' cognitive abilities and problem-solving skills over time, leading to dependence on technology and reduced resilience in face-to-face interactions. Designers must balance the benefits of convenience with the potential risks of over-reliance on unobtrusive design solutions.

While the principle of "Good Design is Unobtrusive" advocates for simplicity, clarity, and user-centeredness in design, it also prompts designers to consider a wide range of factors.

Self-expression

Dieter Rams stresses that good design should not impose itself or draw unnecessary attention. It should seamlessly integrate into the user's life and environment without causing disruption or inconvenience. However, it is important to consider the inherent human desire for self-expression and the role of products in shaping personal identity. Brands often capitalize on this aspect by offering products that help users stand out and create a sense of individuality.

An excellent example of this is the iPod, particularly the distinctive white earphone cables that accompanied it. While the iPod itself remained concealed within users' pockets, the visible white earphone cables became a recognizable symbol associated with the device. In a sea of black earphone cables, the white cables instantly drew attention and signalled to others that the person was using an iPod. This created a cool factor and established a sense of identity for iPod users.

Similarly, certain brands have ventured into the market of expensive gym clothes that can be worn outside of the gym. These clothes are designed not only for their functionality during workouts but also with attention to style and fashion. By wearing these garments in everyday life, individuals can showcase their dedication to fitness and demonstrate a particular lifestyle or image they wish to project. In this case, the design of the gym clothes goes beyond mere functionality and integrates elements that help users stand out and market themselves.

While the principle of unobtrusiveness suggests that products should blend seamlessly into users' lives, it is crucial to acknowledge that some designs can intentionally draw attention and serve as a means of self-expression. By enabling users to stand out or communicate their affiliation with a specific brand or lifestyle, these products cater to a fundamental aspect of human nature — the desire for identity and individuality.

Therefore, it can be argued that in certain cases, a design that deliberately stands out and helps users market themselves has a higher likelihood of success. By aligning with users' aspirations and offering them a means of self-expression, these products tap into powerful psychological factors that drive consumer behaviour. However, it is essential to strike a balance between being attention-grabbing and maintaining usability, as a design that is too obtrusive or impractical may hinder the overall user experience and limit long-term success.

Apple AirPods

An example of a successful product that incorporates obtrusive design elements is the Apple AirPods. While the AirPods themselves are sleek and minimalist in design, their success lies in the integration of certain features and functionalities that can be considered obtrusive in some contexts.

Here's how Apple AirPods demonstrate obtrusive design:

1. **Visible Design**: The AirPods feature a distinctive design with protruding stems that extend downwards from the user's ears. Unlike traditional wired earphones or headphones that blend into the user's attire, the AirPods' design is conspicuous and easily recognizable, drawing attention to the user's ears.

2. **Status Symbol**: Apple has effectively positioned AirPods as a status symbol and fashion accessory, further accentuating their obtrusive nature. The iconic white casing and sleek design serve as a visual indicator of the user's affiliation with the Apple ecosystem and their willingness to embrace cutting-edge technology.

3. **Social Signaling**: Wearing AirPods can signal social status, technological savvy, and adherence to contemporary trends. The visibility of AirPods in public spaces acts as a form of social signalling, conveying a message of modernity and sophistication to others.

4. **Audio Transparency**: The AirPods Pro introduced a feature called "Transparency Mode," which uses external-facing microphones to amplify ambient sounds, making users more aware of their surroundings. While this feature enhances safety and situational awareness, it also

introduces an obtrusive element by blending external sounds with audio playback.

5. **Gesture Controls**: AirPods feature touch-sensitive controls that allow users to adjust volume, skip tracks, or activate Siri with simple gestures. While these controls enhance convenience and usability, they also introduce a visible and tactile interface that may be considered obtrusive in certain contexts.

Despite incorporating obtrusive design elements, Apple AirPods have achieved remarkable success due to their innovative features, seamless integration with Apple devices, and strong brand appeal. The combination of sleek aesthetics, advanced technology, and social signaling has contributed to AirPods' popularity and widespread adoption among consumers.

Rolex Submariner

Another example of a successful product with obtrusive design elements is the Rolex Submariner watch.

Here's how the Rolex Submariner demonstrates obtrusive design:

1. **Distinctive Appearance**: The Rolex Submariner features a bold and robust design with a large, easily recognizable case and prominent crown guards. Its rugged yet elegant aesthetic makes it stand out on the wrist, commanding attention and conveying a sense of prestige and durability.

2. **Branding and Logo**: The Rolex crown logo, prominently displayed on the watch face and crown, serves as a symbol of luxury and craftsmanship. The logo's visibility adds to the watch's obtrusive nature, acting as a subtle form of branding and status assertion.

3. **Bezel and Dial Details**: The Submariner's unidirectional rotating bezel and luminous hour markers provide functional enhancements for divers and adventurers. However, these features also contribute to the watch's obtrusiveness, making it visually distinct and instantly recognizable in

any setting.

4. **Size and Weight**: The Submariner is known for its substantial size and weight, which adds to its presence on the wrist. While larger watch sizes may be considered obtrusive to some, they appeal to others who prefer a bold and masculine aesthetic.

5. **Water Resistance**: As a dive watch, the Submariner boasts impressive water resistance and durability, with features like a screw-down crown and caseback. While these elements enhance the watch's functionality and reliability, they also contribute to its obtrusive design by emphasizing its purpose-built nature.

Despite its obtrusive design elements, the Rolex Submariner has become an iconic timepiece coveted by collectors and enthusiasts worldwide. Its blend of luxury, performance, and heritage appeal resonates with individuals who value precision engineering and timeless style. The Submariner's obtrusive design elements serve as symbols of craftsmanship and status, reinforcing its position as a cornerstone of horological excellence.

Aeron Chair

The Aeron chair is an excellent example of a product that defied conventional expectations and successfully captured attention through its unique design. When it was first launched, the Aeron chair stood out prominently from the typical cushy, upholstered chairs that people were accustomed to. Its distinctive appearance, featuring a modern and ergonomic design with a mesh backrest and sleek lines, immediately grabbed the attention of passersby.

The unconventional design of the Aeron chair was so attention-grabbing that it even led to instances where cars applied sudden brakes in front of the shop where it was displayed. This visual impact created a sense of curiosity and intrigue among viewers. Human nature dictates that people are naturally drawn to fill in the gaps of their curiosity, which worked to the advantage of the Aeron chair. The unique design acted as a conversation starter and compelled people to approach the salesperson to inquire about the chair.

By deviating from the traditional concept of what a chair should look like, the Aeron chair sparked interest and generated a significant amount of buzz. Its distinctiveness helped it to stand out in a crowded market, attracting thousands of customers without requiring excessive marketing efforts.

The Aeron chair's design was deliberately crafted to capture attention and create a memorable impression. By deviating from the norm, it tapped into the human inclination to seek novelty and experience something different. This approach worked exceptionally well for the Aeron chair, as it generated a sense of intrigue and curiosity that enticed customers to engage with the product.

In conclusion, the principle of "Good Design is Unobtrusive" highlights the importance of designing products that seamlessly integrate into users' lives without imposing unnecessary distractions or disruptions. While unobtrusive design fosters usability, simplicity, and user-centricity, there are instances where obtrusive elements can contribute to a product's success, emphasizing branding, functionality, or aesthetic appeal. Striking the right balance between unobtrusive design and purposeful visibility is key to creating products that resonate with users while fulfilling their needs and preferences effectively.

* * *

09 -Good Design is as Little Design as Possible

Dieter Rams' principle of "Good Design is as Little Design as Possible" emphasizes the idea that effective design should be minimalist, stripping away unnecessary elements to focus solely on what is essential for functionality and user experience. This principle advocates for simplicity, clarity, and economy in design, rejecting unnecessary ornamentation or complexity that could detract from the product's purpose and usability.

At its core, this principle encourages designers to distill their designs down to their most fundamental elements, eliminating any superfluous features or embellishments that do not contribute directly to the product's function or user experience. By prioritizing simplicity and restraint, designers can create products that are intuitive, elegant, and timeless.

Rams believed that excessive ornamentation or complexity in design not only adds visual clutter but also hinders usability and detracts from the product's overall effectiveness. Instead, he advocated for designs that are straightforward, honest, and unpretentious, allowing users to engage with the product effortlessly and intuitively.

Furthermore, embracing minimalism in design can lead to greater sustainability by reducing waste, energy consumption, and environmental impact associated with production and consumption. By focusing on essential features and materials, designers can create products that are more efficient, durable, and environmentally friendly.

The principle "Good Design is as Little Design as Possible" may seem conflicting with other design principles, particularly those advocating for thoroughness and attention to detail. While minimalism emphasizes simplicity and the removal of unnecessary elements, other principles like thoroughness down to the last detail emphasize the importance of meticulous craftsmanship and consideration of every aspect of the design.

However, these principles can coexist harmoniously within the design process. The key lies in striking the right balance between simplicity and detail, ensuring that every element of the design serves a purpose and contributes meaningfully to the overall user experience.

For example, while minimalism may call for the removal of extraneous features or ornamentation, thoroughness down to the last detail ensures that the remaining elements are executed with precision and care. By prioritizing essential features and refining them to their most basic and intuitive forms, designers can create products that are both minimalist and meticulously crafted.

In essence, "Good Design is as Little Design as Possible" states that by stripping away the non-essential, designers can achieve clarity, elegance, and enduring relevance in their designs.

Now, let's proceed with the critique of this principle.

The Critique

The principle "Good Design is as Little Design as Possible," also invites critique and raises several considerations:

1. **Risk of Oversimplification**: One critique is that striving for minimalism may lead to oversimplification, where essential features or functionalities are sacrificed in the pursuit of simplicity. Designers may remove elements that are critical for user understanding or functionality, resulting in a design that lacks depth or fails to meet user needs adequately. It can also lead to poor user experience.

2. **Subjectivity of Minimalism**: The concept of minimalism is subjective and can vary based on cultural, aesthetic, and contextual factors. What may be considered minimalist in one context may not necessarily resonate with users or meet their expectations in another. Designers must navigate these diverse perspectives to ensure that minimalism enhances, rather than detracts from, the user experience.

3. **Balance with Functionality**: While minimalism emphasizes simplicity, it is essential to balance this with functionality and usability. Removing design elements indiscriminately can compromise the clarity of communication or the ease of interaction, leading to confusion or frustration among users. Designers must carefully consider the trade-offs between simplicity and functionality to create designs that are intuitive and effective.

4. **Risk of Under-Designing**: In some cases, the pursuit of minimalism may result in under-designing, where the design lacks sufficient detail, depth, or personality to engage users effectively. Minimalist designs that are overly sparse or generic may fail to capture users' attention or evoke an emotional response, diminishing the overall impact of the design.

5. **Complexity of Simplicity**: Achieving simplicity in design can be deceptively complex and challenging. It requires careful consideration of hierarchy, typography, layout, and visual elements to communicate information effectively and facilitate intuitive interaction. Designers must invest time and effort in refining the details of minimalist designs to ensure clarity and coherence.

6. **User Engagement and Delight**: Minimalist designs run the risk of being perceived as sterile or uninspired if they lack elements that engage or delight users. Designers must strike a balance between simplicity and creativity, finding opportunities to introduce subtle details or surprises that enhance the user experience without overwhelming simplicity.

7. **Adaptability and Flexibility**: Minimalist designs may lack the flexibility to accommodate diverse user needs or evolving requirements over time. Designers must anticipate potential changes or variations in user behavior and preferences and design solutions that can adapt accordingly.

A design that is too minimalist may struggle to accommodate these shifts effectively.

8. **Brand Identity and Differentiation**: While minimalism can help stream-line design and communication, it may also undermine efforts to estab-lish a distinctive brand identity or differentiate products from competi-tors. Designers must strike a balance between simplicity and branding, ensuring that minimalist designs remain aligned with the brand's values, personality, and visual identity.

9. **Cultural Considerations**: Minimalist design principles may not resonate equally across different cultures and regions. Some cultures may prefer ornate or decorative design elements that convey richness and tradition, while others may prioritize simplicity and understatement. Designers must consider cultural nuances and preferences when applying minimal-ist design principles in diverse contexts.

10. **Context Dependency:** In certain industries or contexts, the concept of "as little design as possible" may not be suitable or effective. For example, in the realm of advertising and marketing, visual impact and attention-grabbing designs are crucial to capture the audience's attention and communicate messages effectively. In these cases, a more minimalist approach may not achieve the desired impact and may be overshadowed by more visually engaging designs. Minimalist designs may excel in certain contexts, such as digital interfaces or product packaging, but they may be ill-suited for contexts that require richer, more immersive experiences, such as multimedia content or architectural spaces.

11. **Evolution of Design Trends**: Design trends evolve over time, and what constitutes "good design" may vary depending on prevailing aesthetic preferences, technological advancements, and cultural shifts. While minimalism remains a timeless and enduring design principle, designers must remain adaptable and open to evolving trends and paradigms in the design landscape.

It is essential to avoid oversimplification that compromises usability or fails to resonate with the intended audience. By critically evaluating and adapting this principle, designers can create effective and user-centred designs.

Porsche 911

The Porsche 911 sports car, while rooted in a design philosophy of simplicity and functionality, has evolved over the years to incorporate features and technologies that may appear to contradict the principle of "Good design is as Little Design as Possible." Here's how the Porsche 911 has departed from minimalist design principles while still achieving remarkable success:

1. **Technological Advancements**: Modern iterations of the Porsche 911 boast a plethora of advanced technologies aimed at enhancing performance, safety, and convenience. These include features like adaptive cruise control, lane-keeping assist, touchscreen infotainment systems, and advanced driver assistance systems. While these technologies add complexity to the overall design and functionality of the vehicle, they also contribute to a more sophisticated driving experience and appeal to a broader range of consumers who seek modern amenities in their vehicles.

2. **Increased Comfort and Convenience**: Unlike the early iterations of the Porsche 911, which prioritized lightweight construction and driving dynamics above all else, newer models have placed greater emphasis on comfort and convenience features. These include amenities such as heated and ventilated seats, premium audio systems, smartphone integration, and customizable interior options. While these features may seem like unnecessary embellishments from a minimalist standpoint, they cater to the demands of luxury-oriented consumers and enhance the overall driving experience.

3. **Expanded Model Range**: Over the years, Porsche has expanded the 911 lineup to include various model variants and configurations to appeal to different market segments. This diversification has led to the introduction of all-wheel-drive models, turbocharged variants, and

high-performance GT3 and GT2 models, each offering unique features and performance characteristics. While this expansion may dilute the purity of the original 911 concept, it has enabled Porsche to reach a broader audience and maintain its position as a leading manufacturer of high-performance sports cars.

4. **Aesthetic Evolution**: While the fundamental design principles of the Porsche 911 have remained largely consistent throughout its history, the car has undergone subtle aesthetic changes and updates with each new generation. These updates include revisions to the exterior styling, interior layout, and aerodynamic enhancements to improve performance and visual appeal. While some purists may argue that these changes detract from the timeless simplicity of the original design, they have helped keep the 911 fresh and relevant in a competitive market.

5. **Exterior Design:** The Porsche 911 incorporates various exterior design cues that evoke a sense of heritage and performance. These include the distinctive round headlights, sloping roofline, muscular rear fenders, and iconic silhouette that have become synonymous with the 911 brand. While these elements may not directly impact the car's performance, they play a crucial role in defining its visual identity and distinguishing it from other sports cars on the market.

Despite these departures from minimalist design principles, the Porsche 911 has remained one of the most iconic and desirable sports cars in the world. Its ability to balance technological innovation with timeless design aesthetics has contributed to its enduring appeal and success. By embracing advancements in technology, expanding its model range, and evolving its aesthetic design language, the Porsche 911 has demonstrated that good design can encompass a range of features and functionalities without compromising its core identity and appeal.

Samsung Galaxy Fold smartphone

Another example that challenges the principle "Good Design is as Little Design as Possible" is the Samsung Galaxy Fold smartphone.

1. **Foldable Display Technology**: The Samsung Galaxy Fold introduces a revolutionary foldable display technology that allows the smartphone's screen to fold in half, transforming it from a compact device into a larger tablet-like interface. This innovative feature adds complexity to the design, requiring intricate mechanisms to ensure durability and smooth operation. The foldable display technology represents a departure from the simplicity of traditional smartphone designs, introducing new engineering challenges and potential points of failure.

2. **Multi-Functional Design**: The Galaxy Fold aims to offer users a multi-functional device that combines the portability of a smartphone with the productivity of a tablet. In pursuit of this goal, Samsung incorporated additional features and capabilities into the Galaxy Fold, such as multitasking capabilities and enhanced productivity apps. While these features expand the device's functionality, they also contribute to increased complexity in terms of software integration and user interface design.

3. **Complex Hinge Mechanism**: The hinge mechanism of the Samsung Galaxy Fold is a critical component that enables the device to fold and unfold seamlessly. Samsung engineers had to develop a robust hinge mechanism capable of withstanding thousands of folding cycles without compromising the structural integrity of the device. The design and implementation of the hinge mechanism required meticulous attention to detail and extensive testing to ensure reliability and longevity.

4. **User Experience Considerations**: Despite its advanced technology and complex design, Samsung prioritized user experience in the development of the Galaxy Fold. The device features intuitive software features and user interface optimizations to enhance usability and accessibility for a wide range of users. However, the introduction of a foldable display

presented new challenges in terms of user interaction and ergonomics, requiring Samsung to innovate in areas such as app continuity and adaptive display modes.

5. **Premium Aesthetic**: Samsung positioned the Galaxy Fold as a premium flagship device, targeting consumers who value cutting-edge technology and innovative design. The device boasts a sleek and futuristic aesthetic, featuring premium materials and finishes that convey a sense of luxury and sophistication. While the premium aesthetic enhances the device's appeal to discerning consumers, it also adds complexity to the design and manufacturing process, requiring meticulous craftsmanship and attention to detail.

The Samsung Galaxy Fold exemplifies a departure from the principle of minimalist design by embracing advanced technology, multi-functional capabilities, and premium aesthetics. While the device offers groundbreaking innovation and unique features, its complexity presents challenges in terms of engineering, manufacturing, and user experience. Despite these challenges, the Galaxy Fold represents a bold step forward in the evolution of smartphone design and demonstrates Samsung's commitment to pushing the boundaries of innovation in the mobile industry.

Apple vs Microsoft

In the early days of personal computing, Apple's Macintosh computers were known for their sleek and minimalist design. The Macintosh had a user-friendly graphical user interface (GUI) and emphasized simplicity in both hardware and software design. It focused on providing a streamlined and intuitive user experience.

On the other hand, Microsoft's Windows-based PCs offered a more open platform that allowed for greater customization and flexibility. PC manufacturers could add various hardware components and software features to differentiate their products. This often led to PCs being perceived as having an "overly designed" appearance with multiple buttons, ports, and visible components.

Despite the Macintosh's minimalistic design and intuitive user interface, Windows-based PCs gained a significant market share over time. One of the reasons for this was the perceived flexibility and customization options that PCs offered. Users had the freedom to choose from a wide range of hardware configurations and software applications, tailoring their PCs to their specific needs.

Additionally, PC manufacturers started to focus on aesthetics and design, introducing visually striking cases, colourful keyboards, and other eye-catching elements. While these design choices were often criticized for being overly designed or visually cluttered, they appealed to a broader audience who valued personalization and the ability to showcase their individuality through their computing devices.

Over time, the PC market, with its diverse and customizable options, gained traction, and Windows-based PCs became the dominant force in the industry. The Macintosh, with its minimalist design philosophy and limited customization options, faced challenges in attracting a broader market share.

This example highlights how a product with little design, such as the early Macintosh computers, can face competition from products that offer more visually elaborate and customizable options. It emphasizes the importance of considering user preferences, customization capabilities, and market trends when evaluating the effectiveness of minimalistic design versus overly designed features in a product's success.

Traditional vs Digital Cameras

Traditional film cameras were known for their simplicity and straightforward functionality. They had minimal controls and relied on physical film rolls to capture and store images. The design was focused on providing a basic mechanism for taking photos without much emphasis on additional features or user interface.

However, with the advent of digital cameras, the landscape of photography changed drastically. Digital cameras offered numerous advantages over traditional film cameras, including instant image preview, the ability to delete and retake photos, and the convenience of storing images digitally without the need for physical film.

Digital cameras introduced a more complex and feature-rich design. They incorporated LCD screens for image review, various shooting modes and settings, manual controls, and digital image processing capabilities. The user interface became more elaborate, with menus, buttons, and controls to navigate through the camera's functions.

While traditional film cameras had their appeal in terms of simplicity and the nostalgic experience of film photography, the advancements in digital camera design brought about a revolution in the photography industry. The ability to instantly view and review photos, adjust settings, and experiment with different shooting modes expanded the creative possibilities for photographers.

Additionally, digital cameras provided the convenience of easily transferring and sharing images through computer interfaces and online platforms. They also allowed for post-processing and editing of images directly within the camera or on a computer, further enhancing the user experience.

The shift towards digital cameras with their advanced features and user-friendly interfaces led to a decline in the popularity of traditional film cameras. The convenience, flexibility, and versatility offered by digital cameras, along with their visually appealing and feature-rich designs, captured the attention of consumers and professionals alike.

This example demonstrates how a product with little design, like traditional film cameras, can be overtaken by a product with overly designed features, such as digital cameras.

In conclusion, while the principle "Good Design is as Little Design as Possible" advocates for simplicity and minimalism, numerous examples demonstrate the success and innovation that can arise from embracing complexity and pushing the boundaries of conventional design norms. Products like the

Porsche 911, Samsung Galaxy Fold, and various examples from the technology industry challenge the notion that less design is always better. By carefully balancing simplicity with functionality, creativity, and user experience considerations, designers can create products that resonate with consumers and stand the test of time in an ever-evolving marketplace.

* * *

10 -Good Design is Environmentally Friendly

Dieter Rams' principle of "Good Design is Environmentally Friendly" underscores the importance of considering environmental impact throughout the design process. This principle reflects a growing awareness of environmental sustainability and the need for designers to minimize the ecological footprint of their products.

At its core, this principle advocates for designs that prioritize resource efficiency, renewable materials, energy conservation, and waste reduction. It encourages designers to assess the lifecycle of their products, from raw material extraction to manufacturing, distribution, use, and disposal, and to identify opportunities for environmental optimization at each stage.

Key elements of environmentally friendly design include:

1. **Material Selection**: Choosing materials that are renewable, recyclable, biodegradable, or sustainably sourced helps reduce environmental impact. Designers should avoid materials that are toxic, non-recyclable, or environmentally harmful.

2. **Energy Efficiency**: Designing products to be energy-efficient during use helps minimize carbon emissions and reduce energy consumption. This can involve optimizing product performance, reducing power requirements, and incorporating energy-saving features.

3. **Minimalist Design**: Simplifying product design and reducing unnecessary components can help conserve resources and minimize waste.

By focusing on essential functionality and eliminating excess features, designers can create products that are leaner and more sustainable.

4. **Durability and Longevity**: Designing products to be durable, repairable, and long-lasting promotes sustainability by extending product lifespan and reducing the need for frequent replacements. This approach helps minimize resource consumption and waste generation over time.

5. **End-of-Life Considerations**: Designing products with end-of-life considerations in mind, such as ease of disassembly, recyclability of components, and biodegradability of materials, facilitates responsible disposal and recycling practices.

6. **Packaging and Logistics**: Minimizing packaging materials, using eco-friendly packaging options, and optimizing logistics to reduce carbon emissions from transportation contribute to environmental sustainability.

7. **Lifecycle Assessment**: Conducting lifecycle assessments and environmental impact analyses helps designers understand the full environmental footprint of their products and identify areas for improvement.

In summary, "Good Design is Environmentally Friendly" emphasizes the need for designers to integrate environmental considerations into every aspect of the design process, from material selection and manufacturing to distribution, use, and disposal. By prioritizing sustainability, designers can create products that not only meet user needs but also minimize ecological harm and contribute to a more environmentally conscious society.

The Critique

As I reflect on the principle of "Good Design is Environmentally Friendly," I find myself hesitant to critique it. Environmental sustainability is a fundamental aspect of responsible design, and striving to minimize the ecological footprint of products should be a priority for designers. In today's world, where climate change and environmental degradation pose significant threats, it is imperative that designers embrace this principle wholeheartedly.

Rather than critiquing the principle itself, I believe it is more constructive to emphasize the importance of taking proactive measures to integrate environmental considerations into the design process. Designers should view environmental sustainability as a guiding principle that informs every decision they make, from material selection to manufacturing processes and end-of-life considerations.

By embracing environmentally friendly design practices, designers can contribute to the preservation of natural resources, reduction of pollution, and overall improvement of environmental health. Moreover, environmentally friendly design can also lead to innovations that drive economic growth and promote social well-being.

In conclusion, I stand in support of the principle of "Good Design is Environmentally Friendly" and encourage designers to strive for sustainability in all aspects of their work. It is not only a moral imperative but also a practical necessity in building a more sustainable and resilient future for generations to come.

However, achieving environmental friendliness requires a holistic approach beyond the design stage.

1. **Manufacturing Processes:** Designing products to be environmentally friendly often requires implementing sustainable manufacturing processes. However, these processes can be costly and may require significant investments in technology and infrastructure. Manufacturers may be hesitant to adopt such processes due to the initial high costs involved, especially if they operate in price-sensitive markets. This could lead to compromises in sustainability and favouring more traditional, cost-effective manufacturing methods.

2. **Material Selection:** Choosing eco-friendly materials is an essential aspect of environmentally friendly design. However, some environmentally friendly materials may not possess the same durability, performance, or aesthetic qualities as conventional materials. This can lead to com-

promises in the overall quality and longevity of the product, potentially impacting customer satisfaction and the product's market viability.

3. **Consumer Preferences and Market Demand:** While there is a growing awareness and demand for eco-friendly products, it is important to consider consumer preferences and market dynamics. Some consumers may prioritize other factors such as price, brand, or features over the environmental impact of a product. This can create challenges for designers and manufacturers who strive to prioritize sustainability in their products. If the market demand for environmentally friendly products is not strong enough, it can hinder the adoption and success of such designs.

4. **Limited Impact:** Designing a single product to be environmentally friendly does not address the broader systemic issues contributing to environmental degradation. It is crucial to consider the entire lifecycle of a product, including extraction, manufacturing, distribution, use, and end-of-life disposal. Environmental sustainability requires systemic changes that go beyond individual product design, including changes in consumer behaviour, industry practices, and government regulations.

5. **Trade-Offs and Compromises:** Designing products to be environmentally friendly often involves trade-offs and compromises. For example, incorporating recyclable or biodegradable materials may require additional resources, energy, or processes that offset the environmental benefits. Additionally, certain design features that enhance sustainability, such as energy-efficient components, may increase the complexity and cost of the product. Balancing environmental considerations with other design constraints and requirements can be a challenging task.

6. **Supply Chain Management:** An environmentally friendly design should consider the entire supply chain, from sourcing raw materials to delivering the finished product to the end consumer. This includes evaluating the sustainability practices of suppliers, reducing transportation-related emissions through efficient logistics, and minimizing waste generated during production and distribution.

7. **Energy Efficiency:** Designers need to consider the energy consump-

tion of the product throughout its lifecycle. This involves optimizing energy efficiency during the manufacturing process and minimizing energy requirements during product use. Energy-efficient components, power management systems, and low-power consumption modes can contribute to reducing the overall environmental impact.

8. **Packaging:** Packaging plays a significant role in environmental sustainability. Designers should aim to minimize packaging materials, prioritize recyclable or compostable packaging, and reduce excess packaging waste. Additionally, considering the transportation efficiency and space utilization of packaging can help reduce carbon emissions associated with transportation.

9. **Product Durability and Repairability:** Creating products that are durable and repairable can significantly contribute to environmental friendliness. Designing for longevity encourages consumers to use products for longer periods, reducing the need for frequent replacements. Incorporating modular designs and easily replaceable parts can also extend the product's lifespan and reduce waste generation.

10. **End-of-Life Considerations:** Designers should think about the product's end-of-life management, including options for recycling, repurposing, or proper disposal. Designing for disassembly can make it easier to separate components and materials for recycling. Promoting take-back programs or facilitating the recycling process can encourage consumers to dispose of products responsibly.

11. **User Education and Behaviour:** Environmental friendliness also depends on how consumers use and maintain the product. Designers can contribute to sustainability by providing clear instructions, promoting energy-efficient practices, and encouraging responsible product use. Educating users about the environmental impact of their choices can help drive behaviour change and promote more sustainable habits.

12. **Regulatory Compliance:** Designers must consider and comply with environmental regulations and standards applicable to their products. This includes restrictions on hazardous substances, waste management requirements, energy efficiency standards, and emissions control.

To truly achieve environmental friendliness, a holistic approach is necessary, involving collaboration among designers, manufacturers, suppliers, policy-makers, and consumers. Designers must consider the entire lifecycle of the product, from material sourcing to end-of-life disposal, and address environmental challenges at each stage. This requires active involvement beyond the design process, including advocating for sustainable practices, engaging with stakeholders, and embracing continuous improvement initiatives.

* * *

Conclusion

As we conclude our exploration of Dieter Rams' ten principles of good design and their critiques, it is evident that these principles serve as invaluable guidelines for designers striving to create impactful and meaningful products. Each principle encapsulates a fundamental aspect of design philosophy, from innovation and simplicity to environmental sustainability and user-centeredness.

Throughout our journey, we have examined real-world examples that challenge these principles, highlighting design's dynamic and evolving nature in response to technological advancements, cultural shifts, societal needs, etc. From Apple's iconic products to the challenges faced by traditional industries, we have witnessed the intersection of design theory and practice, where principles are tested and redefined in the crucible of real-world application.

As designers, it is essential to embrace these principles as pillars of inspiration and guidance, anchoring our creative endeavours in principles that prioritize functionality, aesthetics, and user experience. However, it is equally crucial to recognize the limitations and nuances inherent in each principle, understanding that design is a complex and multifaceted discipline that defies rigid dogma.

Therefore, we urge readers to keep an open mind as they navigate the realm of design, to follow the principles with diligence and intentionality, but also to question, challenge, and iterate upon them. Blind adherence to principles can stifle creativity and innovation, limiting our ability to push the boundaries of design excellence.

Instead, let us approach design with humility and curiosity, embracing the fluidity and dynamism that characterize the creative process. Let us seek inspiration from diverse sources, learn from our successes and failures, and adapt our approach to design to meet the evolving needs and aspirations of users.

In doing so, we honour the legacy of Dieter Rams and the principles he espoused while charting a course towards a future where design is not just a reflection of our values and aspirations but a catalyst for positive change in the world.

May we continue to explore, innovate, and create with passion and purpose, guided by the principles of good design and driven by a commitment to excellence and human-centered values.

* * *

About the Author

Shah Mohammed is an accomplished Business Strategy and design-thinking consultant with a passion for innovation and user-centred design. He is the founder of D-Cube Designs, a leading design consultancy based in Chennai, India. With a Master's degree in Design from IIT Kanpur, India, which he obtained in 2004, Shah brings a strong academic background and a wealth of practical experience to his work.

As an Industrial Designer, Shah has played a pivotal role in successfully developing and launching over 300 products across various industries over the past decade. His expertise spans the entire product lifecycle, from conducting in-depth user research to designing intuitive and aesthetically pleasing solutions. Shah's keen understanding of customer needs and his ability to translate them into innovative product designs have earned him a reputation for excellence in the industry.

In addition to his contributions to the field of design, Shah has also established himself as a sought-after Business Strategy consultant. Leveraging his customer-centric approach, he has provided valuable insights and guidance to businesses of all sizes, helping them identify market opportunities, develop effective strategies, and drive growth. His expertise in areas such as branding, emotional branding, creativity techniques, leadership, and building competitive advantages has made him a trusted advisor to CEOs, startup founders, and aspiring entrepreneurs.

Shah is an avid blogger and has been sharing his knowledge and insights through his blog for the past six years. With over four hundred articles covering a wide range of topics, including Branding lessons, Design Thinking, Business Strategy, and Psychology in Business, his blog has become a valuable resource for professionals seeking practical advice and inspiration. The content featured in this book are a curated selection of some of his most impactful blogs, offering readers timeless lessons and actionable strategies.

You can connect with me on:
- ⊕ https://shahmm.medium.com
- 𝕏 https://twitter.com/shahbaba
- 🅕 https://www.linkedin.com/in/shahmm
- ⊘ https://www.d-cubedesigns.com

Also by Shah Mohammed

The Positioning Playbook: The Winning Strategies for Market Dominance

Unlock the secrets to market supremacy with "The Positioning Playbook: The Winning Strategies for Market Dominance." This comprehensive guide dives into the art and science of strategic positioning, revealing the proven strategies that will set your business apart from the competition and propel you to the top of your industry.

Discover the power of positioning, going beyond superficial branding and slogans, to create a deep and lasting impact on your target audience. Learn how to carve out a distinct space in consumers' minds, forging emotional connections and delivering unique value that resonates with their needs and desires.

Throughout the book, readers are introduced to thirteen effective positioning strategies, each serving as a pathway to achieving market dominance and sustainable success.

Boil The Ocean: The Story of World's Amazing Brands

Embark on a captivating journey through the world of iconic brands with "Boil The Ocean: The Story of World's Amazing Brands." This thought-provoking book offers a collection of insightful case studies that delve into the successes, failures, and transformative moments of some of the most renowned brands in history.

With meticulous research and captivating storytelling, "Boil The Ocean" offers valuable insights, timeless lessons, and inspiring narratives that will engage both business enthusiasts and casual readers. Whether you are an entrepreneur, marketer, designer, brand strategist, startup owner, CEO, brand consultant, or simply intrigued by the stories behind the brands we know and love, this book will leave you inspired, informed, and eager to explore the dynamic world of branding and business.

INCEPTION: Unveiling the Secrets of Inspirational Leadership

Unlock the secrets to becoming an exceptional leader with "Inception: Unveiling the Secrets of Inspirational Leadership." This captivating book takes you on a transformative journey, exploring the depths of leadership principles, personal development, strategic skills, decision-making, and cognitive biases that shape influential leaders.

Whether you are an aspiring leader seeking to develop your skills, an experienced executive striving for continuous growth, or someone passionate about unlocking the potential of inspirational leadership, this book is designed to provide you with valuable insights, practical strategies, and thought-provoking perspectives.

The Secret Strategies of Marketing: How Brands Use Cognitive Biases to Win Your Wallet

In a world bombarded by marketing messages, understanding the psychology that underpins consumer behaviour is the ultimate game-changer. Whether you're a marketer, entrepreneur, business owner, or an inquisitive consumer, this book unravels the mysteries behind why certain brands resonate deeply while others remain forgettable.

Your Guide to Cognitive Biases: This comprehensive guide explores a treasure trove of cognitive biases, from the well-known to the lesser-explored, offering profound insights into their applications and impact. From the allure of familiarity to the power of scarcity, you'll journey through a spectrum of biases that influence every purchase decision.

SUB-BRANDING PLAYBOOK: Winning Strategies for Targeted Growth

In this captivating playbook, you'll discover a treasure trove of sub-branding strategies, each chapter unveiling a different secret weapon to unlock targeted growth. From creating sub-brands for demographic segmentation to psychographic targeting and cultural branding, we leave no stone unturned.

The book provides insights into successful sub-branding initiatives through real-world case studies, offering practical, actionable strategies for leveraging sub-brands to achieve targeted growth. By examining the considerations and criteria for developing sub-brands, readers can understand how sub-brands contribute to brand differentiation, customer targeting, and market expansion.

Elevate your brand's position, attract a loyal customer base, and surpass your competition. The Sub-Branding Playbook is your trusted companion on this exciting adventure, offering guidance, inspiration, and a roadmap to targeted growth.

Innovation's Hidden Walls: Uncovering Limitations of Jobs To Be Done, Design Thinking, and the Diffusion of Innovation Model.

In "Innovation's Hidden Walls," we delve deep into the core principles of Jobs To Be Done (JTBD), Design Thinking, and the Diffusion of Innovation Model. While these methodologies have been celebrated for sparking innovation, this book takes a critical look at their limitations. Discover how these walls can restrict your innovation endeavours, and learn how to break through them to truly transform your approach to problem-solving.